One in the Spirit

One in the Spirit
Women and ministry in the church

by

Prophetess G.E. Dixon

authorHOUSE®

AuthorHouse™
1663 Liberty Drive
Bloomington, IN 47403
www.authorhouse.com
Phone: 1-800-839-8640

First published by AuthorHouse   05/03/2011

ISBN: 978-1-4634-0043-9 (sc)
ISBN: 978-1-4634-0042-2 (dj)
ISBN: 978-1-4634-1653-9 (ebk)

Library of Congress Control Number: 2011907132

Printed in the United States of America

Any people depicted in stock imagery provided by Thinkstock are models, and such images are being used for illustrative purposes only.
Certain stock imagery © Thinkstock.

This book is printed on acid-free paper.

Dedication

I'd like to dedicate this book to Jesus Christ whom without it would not have been possible to write and who is the author and finisher of my faith. Also to my beloved husband, Apostle A.K. Dixon an end time preacher like no other and very humble man, who did not give up on me in spite of all of the obstacles that stood in the way of our love and marriage.My children,who are all dear to me and were the reason I pressed through the valley of the shadow of death.To vennie and James Jackson, my parents, who gave me the guts to be an adventurer early in life ; taught all of their children not to walk in fear and who I look forward to seeing again in heaven.To the people who fought hard to hold me down,thank you, for making me strong.

G.E. Dixon

FOREWORD

There are many fears and religous doctrines when it comes to women and the church.In my personal opinion I have seen women apostles,prophetesse s,evangelist,pastors and teachers.Pastor Dixon is one that I have personal knowledge of that has a Five fold gifting. Those that have opposed and even questioned this, soon find themselves changing there minds when they experience the depths of ministry,such as revelation knowledge and the doctrinal truths that are expounded upon when she teaches and preaches.It is not a phenominon or a happenstance. She has just been called to do what she does.And under the anointing, she does it well.Simply stated ,she hears from and obeys God.She has come through a lot of bumps in the road to accept what she has been called to and hopefully this book will help other women who may be confused to be free.

Apostle A.K. Dixon

Contents

Introduction

Serving in the church for years and being a woman in ministry, I wondered why there is such a line of tabu when it comes to the things of God.We have many denominations in the end time church from the practical to the outlandish.It seems we have a denomination to fit every type of mindset;yet we are still behind spiritually and hindered by our own doing.It seems there is a lot of confusion when it comes to roles in ministry and in life relations.Hopefully the revelation through this book will help better explain that a lot of what we think we know is exactly what is causing the problems that may be hindering entire ministries and causing a great deal of difficulties in marriages through confusion and unbelief.

One in the Spirit

Chapter 1

Women and ministry in the church

When I was twenty five years old and married to my husband only two years,God called me as a pastor.Being what I thought was logical,intelligent and having the call of a prophetess already on my life from my mothers womb,I just knew I was hearing from the devil. You see,where we lived there was no such thing as a women calling herself a pastor. And I had already suffered and paid the price as a woman operating in a prophetic gifting.An area that God just happened to allow me to operate in, "by chance",as some put it.So I really was losing it ;to say that he called me to pastor a church.My husband had been in ministry at that time for about twenty years and had pastored,assistant pastored and had been an elder. God called him as an Apostle with an end time teaching and all I would do is complicate everything and upset the order for ministry where we lived.But being stubborn,I decided after confirmation to obey God.Since that time I have not only pastored but traveled and have been a pioneer for others to go forward in ministry by preaching the message of counting up the cost and moving ahead full throttle by the leading of the holyghost.

One in the Spirit

Women and ministry in the church

Chapter one

You might find my use of the word pioneer a bit strange, but it is actually what I found my experience to be. In the year of 1997 I was pastoring a church in the Richmond, IN. area when it seemed we were hit with one of the heaviest warefares ever.The pressure was so great that I literally had to shut the ministry down because a bad seed of discord was sewn in our church.We had a home daycare that I also had to shut down. My husband had gone through a heavy attack and we did not fully recognize what all was happening.I had the strangest couple of visions that I ever had in my life.The only comparison was the very real visitation from Jesus Christ in the year of 1988 when my daughter Von was born.He told me about how he called me to be a prophet and had given me the gift of faith and that he wanted me to use it. He also said that through that gift of faith all of the other gifts would work.He told me more things of my journey to come, but of more importance,he told me to tell the story of his soon coming every where I went and that every time I told the story of his visitation he would back up what I said.And I can tell you with the support of many witnesses that he did and is doing just what he said.Getting back to the two visions I had before the demonic attacks that hit.The first one was when the church was in a great power flow where people were getting really blessed.Some where even coming out of great poverty,sickness and disease and testifying of the goodness of Jesus.I was at home in a deep prayer and fasting season that the Lord had called me into and I went into an open vision where I was standing outside of this old house with porches on each side.It was so old it was falling apart it seemed.Water was gushing out of it on all sides.I was about 12 to 14 feet away from it trying to hold up a preaching robe that I was wearing,so it wouldn't get wet.I had no shoes on my feet and the water was flowing past my feet.

One in the Spirit

Women and ministry in the church

All of a sudden I was past this chain link Fence that was about 6 feet tall that was half standing and half torn down. As if something very large had torn it half away.Suddenly,I looked down and the water was still flowing past my feet and I was standing on a smooth 2 feet wide, flat stone.I heard God's voice telling me to dive in to now what was before me a river flowing down.I was afraid and I said 'Lord,I can't swim'.The Lord said to me "dive in;you will surely not drown".We went over this conversation again and finally with great fear,I jumped into the waterfall going down into this rushing river.As I hit the water an angel with golden blonde hair told me "hurry,hurry,go down,go down and save the man". "Hurry,go down". Her hands was in the praying position.As I went down I saw what appeared to be a man on the bottom of this river, just laying there. I don't know how I was able to breath under all of the water,but I surely did not drown as the Lord had spoken.I immediately laid hands on this man that looked on the verge of death and the vision was over.The second vision was about two weeks later when at my home daycare I fell in a deep sleep at nap time for everyone and I saw the biggest death angel I ever saw in my life.He came in through the back door in this vision and he swept through the daycare with the children in it.And being the prayer warrior that I am,I wanted to get up and attack this spirit,but the Lord would not permit me to.Something like cold honey was being poured into my ear as I helplessly watched this large death angel go through my house,with his pick in his hand and hooded.The icey substance that was being poured in my ear was being put there by the holy ghost.All I can say is that my spiritual senses have been height ened to a level of great purportions,like never before.And the question came after we left this house and moved to Florida for four months where I was miserable;having to leave every thing and all of the things we were familiar with.Why?

One in the Spirit

Women and ministry in the church

This is just a small portion of the many things that happened to me and my family in the year of 1997.I prayed and prayed and really began a deep study in the word of God in the new testament especially.I had no idea God was getting me ready for one of the biggest moves of God we were yet to see.All of the attacks of the enemy was to get me ready for what was a breakout revival in the Bessemer,AL. Area.The place of my birth.This move had been prophesied to me and prayed about.You see,much of my family had gotten healed and delivered and the thing was they were not born again.I was the first women to preach in a church in Brownsville,AL. Where they said it would'nt happen;but God opened the door.We ended up moving to Bessemer,AL.for a season where I watched God beautifully save my father,who people thought would never get saved. He would not join anyones church;but he joined mine and was faithful.You see,the man in the first vision was my dad who just past in October of 2004 and the Lord knew I wanted him to be saved. And let me put it this way ;he was a hard man and God knew it would take a hard word to save him from someone he loved and who he knew that loved him.The man in the vision was not just my dad,but people like him who are hard to reach it seems.The water in the vision represented the spirit of God and his leading.The angel represented things happening quickly and miraculously through the prayers of the righteous.The robe represented a preached prophetic and timely word in season to the saving of souls.I had to dive in, in order to be in the proper timing.The house represented the old order or traditional church and the water coming from under the doorpost represented the old not being able to contain the new thing that God is doing. The fence represented something being kept out. It being torn down by the hand of God so that women could go in ministry into places they have not been allowed to before in the history of the church.

One in the Spirit

Women and ministry in the church

The second vision was totally opposite,yet strangely tied to the first.The death angel represented a death coming to everything that I was familiar with in a big way.It was so large because the personal vision I had for my life and family was so large.I had big dreams for myself and for my family in Richmond.And here comes God,tearing them all away for his purposing in my life.In 1996 a women came to our church and told the ministry that God was going to strip us; to test us.To see where our hearts were. We thought that this women was a false prophet.What she said could not happen,we were in tune with God.Be careful what you ask God for!You might get it! Our ministry did a lot of fasting and praying and warfaring with the devil.We often shut in and some to this day don't understand why. We now know.The cold or icey substance that was put in my ear in the second vision represented a word that was so cold in nature it almost seemed brutish.This was a radical teaching and prophetic preaching that God gave me in the anointing that did not toy with people or tickle there itching ears.God gave it to me about three years before the year of 1997 and even my husband didn't understand the harshness of it.You see,the message God gave me to preach didn't bring peace,but a sword.St. Mt. 10 v. 34 "Think not that I have come to send peace on earth; I came not to send peace,but a sword". This sword that Jesus was speaking of was a word so razor sharp that it would cut to and through the bones of men and women causing conviction to repentance and the saving of their souls. But it wouldn't be to the liking of the messenger;I was and still am a target for backlash and retaliation.There is an awesome price to be paid for telling the truth and not comforting people in their mess.People were even going to my husband trying to get him to somehow "talk to me".To make me not preach such harsh messages.Little did they know.Those so called "harsh messages" is what was getting through to their drug addicted children and husbands, even healing their sick bodies and rebuking the devil from their homes.Zech. 3v. 1 And he showed me Joshua the high priest standing before the angel of the Lord,and Satan standing at his right hand to resist him.

One in the Spirit

Women and ministry in the church

Some people are full of the devil. They don't just have an alcohol problem or mental problems. They are not just hurting from their past or have a drug addiction;they are bound,snared in sin.Caught up and need to be birthed out or born again out of the birth canal of sin.That is why Jesus told Nicademus "you must be born again".Zech. 3 v.2 And the Lord said unto Satan, The Lord rebuke thee,O Satan;even the Lord that hath chosen Jerusalem rebuke thee;is not this a brand plucked out of the fire?This very chapter in the bible is talking about the Lord rebuking satan.The devil is ignorant and he is stubborn like a bad stain.He must be rebuked with the strong word of God. And as the bible states the Lord or the word of the Lord has to rebuke him.It takes a strong word for a strong or stubborn sin or sinner.The chosen Jerusalem is a chosen people;strong in the Lord and ready for battle.Read all of Zech. 3 about the church being restored and enpowered for a great work in the last days. Before we get to our main scriptures I wanted to share these couple of visions and experiences with you to make clear what we're about to reveal about women and ministry.Back to the icey substance that went in my ear.Yes,it was as cold as ice and it went down into my throat,past my tongue and down to my belly.A cold word that would come out as hot as fire.Rev. 3 v.15 I know thy works,that thou art neither cold nor hot;I would thou were cold or hot.2 So then because thou art lukewarm,and neither cold nor hot,I will spue thee out of my mouth.Jesus is saying that he does not want people to straddle the fence.He is saying he wants a consistent church that is able to maintain the anointing and not give in to the blows and pressures of this life.Fire

and ice is maintained at certain degrees of temperature in order to be kept.Ice preserves and fire destroys whatever is in it's path. The word has to be kept in us;God's people, by it being guarded and us seeming cold by not participating in everything the world has to offer and coming out from among them and being separate. The word has to be like fire coming out of our bellies,to burn up everything in the way of the path of holiness and salvation.

One in the Spirit

Women and ministry in the church

I know that comparing fire and ice to some might seem to be a strange comparison,but it is not my comparison it is Jesus's.They both can be very deadly if used the wrong way. They both have the capacity to do damage if not properly handled. So ice can be just as deadly as fire.What am I saying?God does not want us so cold that we do not have any concern about the welfare of others and be unattached from reality;just cold enough to not enter into temptation.At the right temperature fire and ice can both burn and damage.So we have to be at the right degree in order to be effective and accomplish what the holyghost calls us to do.The word that I am speaking of is the word that say's 'yes,I know you are married and the man you are living with is not your husband.But God loves you in spite of that and still wants to save you and is concerned with your needs.'St. John 4 v. 7. Here is this Samaritan women who knew that the Jews had nothing to do with her people and wanted nothing to do with them.The word found her in Jesus at a time when she was not looking for holiness in a get by religion that she could still live in sin in.She found out that the love of God was deeper than what she knew and that it transcended the barrier of race.The word I am talking about goes deep enough to ask do you want to be made whole?It is to a people who feel there is no hope for them.That they have gone too far to be saved or that there condition is so bad they can't be helped. Like the man at the pool of Bethesda that had his condition for 38 years and Jesus stopped by to let him know that God knew about his case and did he really want to be made whole or depend on man for the rest of his life.St. John 5 v.6 . . . Wilt thou be made whole.

One in the Spirit

Women and ministry in the church

There is another factor that comes into play with the type of word that I am talking about.In my own observation I discovered a certain type of personality or mindset that the person or persons that teach this type of message must posses. That is, you have to have a thick skin,holy boldness and an iron jaw.I am not saying you have to be as mean as a snake, just as wise as one.Mt. 10 v. 16 Behold,I send you forth as sheep in the midst of wolves;be ye therefore wise as serpents, and harmless as doves.Jesus was giving an example of a mind set that he wanted the disciples to have.Sheep look a lot dumber than they are and can attack you as well as goat,but because of their mentality they will only attack if they're scared.They would rather go the other way or scatter than fight you and have an easy spirit and an open mind to be lead.Serpents much of the time try to attack prey within their own range that they think they can handle. They know that they are venomous and can deaden their prey. They can hide themselves well.They are willing to take on larger prey if they have to,but only in certain situations such as if they are hungry or threatened.Doves are beautiful creatures that have the ability to take flight at will and can be trained and kept.They are very sensitive to sight and sounds. They are well aware of their environment and will take off at the moment that they feel any sign of danger and by no means will attack.Sheep, serpents and doves.Why would Jesus use such very different animals,with such different characteristics?I believe it is because he was training his desciples to go into a hostile world,preaching a gospel that was virtually new and it wouldn't be accepted by all.So there were certain qualities they had to posses in order to be sustained and successful. Not in the way of a popularity contest,but in the preaching of the gospel and the winning of souls.

One in the Spirit

Women and ministry in the church

I am not saying that we have to be unintelligent farm animals.Please don't get confused what I'm saying.I am saying that you can't approach every situation the same.There have been times when I have gone into churches, with a message I really didn't want to preach. Especially if most of it was to the leadership in the ministry.In these cases, you know that there is a possibility you won't be invited back.There was some occasions when I was put in this position by the holyghost.I went into the situation knowing the word was not going to be something to make everybody laugh and say, "isn't she wonderful"? "Well let's have her back"! This is part of the testing process of being obedient. My point is, I didn't go in there like a linebacker trying to knock the pastor out of the way and anxiously tear up the church.I went in love and taught a rough word and kept a cool demeaner. My intention was not to try to prove the word by beating it down their throats,but to be as accurate and as confident in the holyghost as I possibly could.God got the glory and people were blessed. Sometimes you get invited back,when the leader is strong and has a prophetic ear to hear and know's the confirmation of God. I'm sure you are asking yourself;What does all of this have to do with women and ministry in the church?My answer to you is everything.All of these obstacles that are tools of testing and trials for men, are the same for women and even worser, is the denial of positioning or calling.And this leads us to our scripture of focus as I call it ;that somewhat balances the scales in ministry.Helping us to understand the working of the spirit of of God, identifying purpose and ministry.

One in the Spirit

Chapter two

The common equation of sin

It seems when it comes to sin we have no respect of persons.We don't look at sin like it is something that has a specific gender link.All sin is sin,regardless of who you are or what sex you are.There are female drug addicts and there are male drug addicts.There are female murderers and there are male murderers.There are female adulterers and there are male adulterers. We have no problem associating the sin with people,regardless of gender.Gal. 3 v. 22 But the scripture hath concluded all under sin, that the promise by faith of Jesus Christ might be given to them that believe.So this, our focus scripture,tells us that men and women, boys and girls are not considered separate when it comes to sin. It states that all are under sin.There are other examples that I could use to stress my point and I will to help us better understand where I am coming from.If you were in a serious car accident and you needed a doctor to save your life and the specialist for the surgery was a woman. You would have no problem letting that woman do what she had been trained and qualified to do.You wouldn't even ask to see her credentials.As long as you know that the hospital has approved her and that was where you were brought to receive help.It would be just fine, as long as it would save your life. Well why can't you trust your soul to the anointing on the life of a women who has been trained and qualified by God and called to the ministry by the holyghost.We trivialize the fact that some women are more anointed than men to do a thing in the spirit.And take lightly the fact that women may have a life changing and saving anointing on her life that would benefit all.Just as in the natural there are female doctors who are more skilled than their male counterparts.

One in the Spirit

The common equation of sin

I have asked ten or more male pastors these questions and they all stated that they didn't have problems with women and ministry.One told me as long as they stay in there place.When I asked what place that was? He said that place was as missionaries or in ministries of helps.So they would have something to do and stay out of the way.He had a problem with women as apostles,prophets, evangelists and pastors,but they could teach because the bible said that the old women could teach the younger women. When I asked another he believed that God would let a women co-pastor only if her husband was the pastor.She did not have to be qualified as long as she was the pastors wife.Another believed that women could preach as long as she didn't wear pants, because then she was trying to be like a man and it wasn't ladylike to do such a thing.One other uses the scripture that a women should not be allowed to speak in church.We will address this one later.Let's not just talk about men here;we want to be equal in our summations.I have an aunt who is steeped in tradition and does not believe that women are suppose to preach.She told me; "women don't do such things".She has a daughter that preaches.She also believes that a woman can go in a factory where she lives,sweat like a dog working like a man, earn a living for herself and that's okay.But to pick up a bible and preach is a no,no.I have encountered women in churches for years that are so bound up in their traditions and doctrines until it has become a form of slavery.I knew an older woman who was once highly anointed of God and several of her family members confirmed it.She once pastored a church in the city of Chicago and stepped down because she lost her first husband, who wasn't supportive and intimidating. She remarried and wanted to please her new husband, who took over and tore up the church. She died a sad, crippled old woman and her last words to me was; "stand your ground for God and don't end up like me".It scared obedience into me.I don't believe that the God I know did that to her.I believe her heart was broken for not fulfilling her dream.She told me on numerous occassions of the visitation she had with Jesus and what he called her to do.

One in the Spirit

The common equation of sin

Women are there own worst enemies sometimes. We fight for equality in many areas,yet in the things of God, a lot of us are swayed to the way of what is popular.Bishop Jakes done a beautiful job of loosing us;but to what?What exactly have we been loosed to.Lu. 10 v. 40 But Martha was cumbered about much serving,and came to him,and said, Lord, dost thou not care that my sister has left me to serve alone?Bid her therefore that she help me.41 And Jesus answered and said unto her, Martha,Martha thou art careful and troubled about many things; 42 But one thing is needful;and Mary hath chosen that good part, which shall not be taken away from her.We see here,Mary was not as concerned with doing what was expected of her, as she was with hearing what Jesus had to say.Women are raised with an expectancy to perform womanly duties at all cost in most cultures and there is nothing wrong with being the domestic housewife.But there is a problem when those things overwhelm you to the point when you miss out on the things of God.And yes, we have to be faithful in the things of life,but not to the point of exhaustion and distress.That is why we need time with the Lord. To become focused and centered and full of faith.Mary wasn't trying to blow off her sister;she was trying to put on Christ.That is what Jesus was talking about that could not be taken away. Martha was so use to doing what she had been doing all her life that she did not realize what she was missing out on.Many women have missed and are still missing God because of other roles in life that are expected of them.They don't realize that they can have it all.A husband,children,business and ministry.Ask the woman in pr. 31,the virtuous woman.

One in the Spirit

The common equation of sin

Pr. 31 v. 10 Who can find a virtuous women? This is a big question being asked of king Lemuel concerning things that his mother taught.She wanted him to be a wise ruler and not give his strength to women.In other words,she did not want him to be drained because of choosing the wrong woman to be by his side. She was also letting it be known that his Queen should not be a (trophy wife).There are a lot of women who are performers and not being who they actually are.That is what a (trophy wife) is. I know you are thinking ;what does a (trophy wife) have to do with a virtuous women?Well,it is a sort of stepford wife. You don't necessarily have to be a wife to be one.As I stated earlier;women are programmed to do certain things,according to their culture,a certain way.It is a pressure cooker waiting to explode.And we wonder why heart attacks and heart disease is the number one killer of women.Look at how distressed Martha was,trying to perform.I mean,give me a break,nobody was starving!The virtuous women however,is cool,calm and collected.She knows what time to get dinner started.She serves others besides her family.She is not broke;she has maidens that serve her,but she is not afraid to get her hands dirty.She takes the time to please her man.She knows what he likes.Her children rise up and call her blessed.She makes a mean breakfast.She is a good business women and knows where and how to shop.She doesn't depend on her husband for everything. The girls got skills.The fruit of her hands is mentioned twice in proverbs.She is a very productive women. She respects the sanctity of marriage.She ain't ugly;she knows she's got it going on and doesn't flirt with men because she can.She is respected for being a Godly woman.Wow! What big shoes to fill.Not so big,when we stay at the feet of Jesus. He is our enabler;our way maker.I can do all things through Christ which strengtheneth me Ph. 4 v. 13.

One in the Spirit

The common equation of sin

If you are spiritual at all, I know that you can identify with these women in the bible.We all have weaknesses and strengths.This is true.All I know personally is that I had to rely on God and Godly older women to become the mother and the wife that I am.I have been to the school of hard knocks when it comes to realizing who and whose I am.There are a lot of skills that I have that I know that the holyghost has enabled me to do because I asked him to.People don't always have the answer to your problem.One of my mentors in the Lord said it best,when he said, "everyone is not anointed to hear your problems".Took me a while; but I soon understood what he meant by it.Everybody is not in tune with the holyghost.They won't always have the solution to your marriage problem.We are all different and what works for me won't necessarily work for you.We have to acknowledge God in all of our ways, as the word says,because he is our source. There are a lot of teachings on marriage and what is suppose to work.Yet I discern even some of the ones teaching this stuff.They are common people, like everybody else. We saw a couple teaching one time that stated. "We never argue; as a matter of fact we don't even get angry;we have discussions". Liars,liars,pants on fire.If you have lived with someone any considerable amount of time,you get mad at them because it is human nature. And I have news for some people.We don't walk around in the anointing twenty four hours a day.We have bad days and don't want to be bothered sometimes.When we don't communicate we end up like Martha.Jesus had to call the sisters name twice in order to get her attention.She was talking, but not sharing what she really felt. She in a way was trying to do what she thought was pleasing for others to her own hurt and frustration and she wanted her sister to carry some of the load.Some women are the same way and are losing more than they are gaining.

One in the Spirit

The common equation of Sin

So where are we? We talked about this super woman in proverbs 31. Where does she exist? Is there such a woman? Yes there is. Who can find her? Only God can. I can do all things through Christ that strengthens me. Virtue= strength, manliness, virtue. Conformity to a standard of right.;morality. A particular moral excellence. Manly strength or courage;valor. A commendable quality;merit. Active power to accomplish a given affect;potency,efficacy. Chastity,especially in a women. This is what websters dictionary defines as virtue. This can only come from God. When it is faked it produces perversion. It produces a spirit that we manufacture. This is why we find women preaching like men or carrying themselves in a brutish way. Jesus said without him we can do nothing. And that, my friend is true. What is not of faith is sin as the word of God says. Ro. 14 v. 23. The virtue of God is nothing like some of us think it is. It enables a women to do something beyond her natural strength. She does not have to be mannish to do a manly thing. She can be as sexy as May West and cast out demons. We have a perverted idea of what a strong women looks like in the the eyes of God. The women comes from the man. So by no means should she try to be a man. That's why we have problems in society with lesbianism. It is a spirit of confusion, that women captured by it get caught up in. Most dominant lesbian women have calls on their lives to do works for God and great things in the kingdom. They don't realize that they are trapped in the lie of satan. They are trying to prove to themselves and others that they can be as strong as a man. Thus,a false virtue. The serious danger in this is when this spirit shows up in the church and perverts Godly virtue.

One in the Spirit

The common Equation of sin

Strong words? Well, I told you God did not call me to patty cake in the spirit. The things that we in the church think have nothing to do with the problems we're having are the very root and source of the problems we are having. There is a spirit that can cause women in the church to try to sort of have a take over spirit, when they feel they have no place in ministry. And this is where this dominant spirit can come in as a false virtue also. A false virtue is nothing but a false anointing or false Christ as the bible says. St. Mt. 24 v. 5 For many shall come in my name, saying, I am Christ; and shall deceive many. Satan comes as the bible says, in the form of an angel of light. He's not going to show up in a red suite, with big horns sticking up out of his head, a tail and a pitchfork. That's not his style. To give you an example of what I'm talking about. Some twelve years ago or more; we were attending a church where my husband was in leadership. There was an uproar because some of the women didn't feel validated as ministers. So, there was this one sister who felt because she was older and she had been there a long time, she was going to lead a sort of uprising against the leadership of the church. You see, as I said earlier. There was no such thing as women pastors where we lived and some didn't even believe women could or was called as ministers. She began to recruit other women who felt like they had callings on their lives. She had some influence because we listened to her. She was an anointed and respected woman in the community. She was anointed, but in an angry rage and under the influence of demons. She didn't know sometimes, when it was God using her or the devil. A false virtue or false Christ anointing will blind you like this.She began to heavily attack the men and question their character.This woman once highly esteemed my husband and now it's like she wanted to take his head off. She would criticize the smallest things he did. And the poor pastor didn't have a chance.She wanted to turn the whole church against him.

One in the Spirit

The common equation of sin

Eventually things got out of hand in the ministry because no one really knew how to deal with this spirit of rebellion that became a Jezebel spirit.There were other things that were out of order in the ministry,but they were nowhere near as bad as this thing got.The Lord kept me out of a lot of this after the spirit had already affected me mentally and emotionally.It took years for all of the individuals involved to heal and some never did.The thief comes to steal,kill and destroy as Jesus said.And did he do it in this growing ministry.The pastor was voted out and the church fell apart and has never been the same.This spirit gives place to the misuse of the scriptures we all know so well and that some like to use in order to keep the fences up and the doors closed to women in ministry in many denominations.Let's look at another scripture, that we hear a lot in churches that don't have a clear revelation.Is. 3 v. 12 As for my people,children are their oppressors,and women rule over them,o my people, they which lead thee cause thee to err, and destroy the way of thy paths.The reference scripture for Is. 3 v. 12, according to the Thompson chain addition of the King James bible is 1 k. 11 v. 4 For it came to pass,when Solomon was old,that his wives turned away his heart after other gods; and his heart was not perfect with the Lord his God,as was the heart of David his father.What is being emphasized here is that Solomon's wives turned his heart after other gods.These women where not calling themselves ministers.They were his wives.This type of ruling has nothing to do with a woman who has been anointed of God,for a purpose or calling.When we lose our focus it is easy to appear like Solomon's wives.The dividing factor here, that saves women in a real God ordained ministry is being led and charged by the holyghost.St. Jn.1 v. 12 But as many as received him,to them gave he power to become the sons of God. even to them that believe on his name;13 Which were born,not of blood,nor of the will of the flesh,nor of the will of man,but of God.

One in the Spirit

The common equation of sin

Now in 1k. 11 v. 4 we talked about how Solomon's wives got him to follow after other god's;not that Solomon had a priest or a spiritual leader in the faith of his father David lead him off the beaten path.This was his own lust for his wives that took his eyes off the God of his father.And again I'll point out that these were wives,not ministers.They wouldn't have known the true God from a rock on the ground.So this shows you better of where I'm headed with this.In Is. 3 v. 12 where it talks about women ruling over the men and children being their (the men's) oppressors,it is talking of a lack of order or loss of control,no respect and the men not being allowed to rule at home.And at home a man is the head of the house and he is suppose to have say in what goes on in his house.The bible says that the husband is the head of the wife. Ephes. 5 v. 23 For the husband is the head of the wife,even as Christ is the head of the church;and he is the saviour of the body.So am I saying that a woman is suppose to run the house as if the man was not the head?Even if the husband is wrong, makes mistakes, and he will.It is his responsibility to have a vision for the family.This is his God given or devine assignment.Ephes. 5 v. 24 Therefore as the church is subject unto Christ,so let the wives be to their own husbands in everything.Can you see in this verse that a comparison is being made to wives and their husbands;Christ and the church. The comparison is them being one in agreement and working together. The marriage in the flesh being one of minds,wills and emotions. The word Christ here is speaking of the anointing of the holyghost and us, male and female, being subject to him.Both male and female.

One in the Spirit

The common equation of sin

Let's take a closer look at St. Jn. 1 v. 12 But as many as received him,to them gave he power to become the sons of God,even to them that believe on his name;13 Which were born, not of blood,nor of the will of the flesh,nor of the will of man,but of God.In this 13th verse it say's,born not of blood or not from the womb of a woman. Nor of the will of flesh or not of the approval of mankind. But of God or by God's spirit.This scripture is plainly saying to me that a son of God doesn't necessarily have to be of the male gender. It states the giving of God's power to a people willing to be lead by his spirit.When God ordained me it was from my others womb.He didn't look and say oops,I didn't mean to make you a prophet! You're a girl! Ephes. 4 v. 11 And he gave some,apostles;and some, prophets;and some,evangelists;and some,pastors and teachers; God made no mistakes when he ordained these ministries in heaven. Iv'e heard many women who thought that the callings on their lives was because some man didn't step up to the plate and do the job that they were suppose to do, so God called them as some sort of replacement.I even had people tell me that my husband wasn't ready to step into the placing of a pastor, so God was having me to sort of,stand in the gap and that I would have to step down when he was ready to get in his place.God doesn't make mistakes and is not the author of confusion,so why would he give you a gift and take it back?He is not an indian giver either.Look at what the bible says he gives these gifts for.Ephes. 4 v. 12 For the perfecting of the saints, for the working of the ministry,for the edifying of the body of Christ; For the perfecting of the saints or to bring us to a place where we are fully functioning in our purpose.For the working of the ministry or so that the ministry will flow without hinderance.For the edifying of the body of Christ or instruction and improvement in morality. When it comes to these things of the spirit,they are not relative to gender,only to the anointing. And the anointing of God is the only thing that destroys the yoke of sin.

One in the Spirit

The common equation of sin

let's look at some more scriptures that I ran reference on and how they are being used or misused.I Co. 14 v.34 Let your women keep silence in the churches;for it is not permitted unto them to speak;but they are commanded to be under obedience, as also saith the law.This scripture in 1 Co. 14 is explaining things concerning conjugal or marital matters.It's references are again,Ephes. 5 v. 22 talking of the wives submission and we must understand that a lot of home roles were being established so that the ministry would not be spotted.Another reference is 1 Ti. 2 v. 11 Let the woman learn in silence with all subjection.It was not a big matter for women to be educated,so they asked a lot of questions sitting right in church during the time that the word was being taught.So the men were given instructions to tell their wives to shut up during church and ask questions later.To be honest,we in the end time church sometimes act the same way.

I know that there have been times when I was sitting in church and there would be this annoying person talking all through the service. Several times I've had to physically move in order to hear what was being taught.People sit in anointed services disrespecting the holyghost all the time and don't think anything of it.Well, the women did it back then because as I said, church manners and home lifestyle according to the christian walk was newly being taught back then. We in the end time church are without excuse. Col. 3 v. 18 is another reference scripture. Wives,submit yourselves unto your own husbands,as it is fit in the Lord.As it is fit in the Lord,meaning we don't have to submit to just any old thing that is handed to us.But a Godly submission.It is not a good thing to stay in a situation that is life threatening thinking you can somehow change a person.My point here is that these scriptures refer to marriage.The minister who happens to be a female has to have a home life that shows she is submissive to her husband and a mother to her children.She has to be that virtuous women.Her home life as well as a mans home life has to be in order.This however,is a hard task requiring great restraint and wisdom to those ministers and pew members alike who marry out of the will of God.Or those who are unequally yoked in a time when even Godly marriages are failing because of the pressures of life.

One in the Spirit

The common equation of sin

1 Pe. 3 v. 1 Likewise, ye wives, be in subjection to your own husbands;that,if any obey not the word,they may also without the word be won by the conversation of the wives.This is the perfect scripture for what we are talking about.It tells the saved wife that even with an unbelieving husband.Who she is able to communicate with, can be won without the word of God being preached to them.The bible says, he who wins souls is wise.These verses of scripture are saying that she, by her(conversation) or lifestyle,can win her husband to the Lord.This scripture goes on to say that it has nothing to do with the clothing that the woman wears or how she wears her hair.This is a scripture that has freed a lot of women from what I call clothesline bondage.Clothesline bondage is where you are defined by the kind of clothes that you wear.In a lot of denominations, we say that there is a certain way that a women has to dress before we can say that she is a Godly woman.Men don't go through this in most denominations.This also is a pressure that is placed on most women.I am not saying that we are to dress like tarts.We,hopefully will have some kind of tact when it comes to what we wear.On the other hand,I have seen women who say they are saved with everything hanging out that shouldn't be showing. We should not use our liberty as an occasion to sin as the bible says.1 Pe. 3 v. 3 Whose adorning let it not be that outward adorning of plaiting the hair,and of wearing of gold,or of putting on of apparel.There are denominations that promote the more gold and the more fancy clothes you have,the more you will seem to be blessed or saved.1 Pe. 3 v. 4 But let it be the hidden man of the heart,in that which is not corruptible,even the ornament

of a meek and quiet spirit,which is in the sight of God of great price.Spirit= a life giving force;the animating principle;soul. Have you ever heard anyone say that someone had a good soul?The word of God is saying here to that woman dealing with an unbelieving husband to win him by having a good soul and fearing or reverencing God by respecting the things of God.This woman can be what her husband needs and still be effective in the kingdom as an Esther.

One in the Spirit

The common equation of sin

These obstacles when it comes to life in the church and ministry can be easily avoided if we wait on God in life matters such as marriage. There is one scripture in the bible that fare warns us about trying to be one with people who are not saved. 2nd Co. 6 v. 14 Be ye not unequally yoked with unbelievers;for what fellowship hath righteousness with unrighteousness?This is why I said it takes a great deal of restraint and wisdom dealing with an individual who is not born again.Especially when we are called into ministry. The devil is already using everything he can to hinder and even stop the anointing from going forward in marriages that are so called (equally yoked),so we better believe it is even harder for a woman to call herself a minister and be in a marriage where the person does not only have problems believing in the things of God;but they have a problem believing in you as a minister.This piece of scripture goes on to ask. . . . and what communion hath light with darkness?The bible says that darkness cannot comprehend light.Darkness can't understand light. So you are literally in two different worlds;with two different forms of communication.That mans source is the things of this world and he gets all of his resources and information from what is in the world. That is what he has depended on all of his life and you come along and tell him that everything he has relied on is false and fading away. It takes a great deal of patience to birth someone out of darkness that is so close to you sharing a marriage bed and preach to the nations, be effective and keep a cool head.Iv'e heard some women say it is like they are raising another child because of the lack of understanding.2nd Co. 6 v. 15 And what concord hath

Christ with belial? Or what part hath he that believeth with an infidel?Belial= misrepresent.2 to show something to be false. To run counter to.

One in the Spiritual

The common equation of sin

This word is a discriptive of how satan works. As we see, he is a liar and the father of all lies as the word says. Anyone, no matter how good of a person they are,that is not born again can't see the kingdom and it is hard to believe in something you can't see.We can only see the kingdom in the spirit and if you have not the spirit of God you can not see it.Infidel=one who is not a christian or opposes christianity.So infidels completely oppose christianity. It is already a balancing act at times for me personally in order to be married to a christian man and deal with the blows and pressures of life.My hat goes off to those who can maintain a marriage to a man that knows nothing about the christian experience.This scripture goes on to talk about coming out from among them and being separate. God is also saying down further that then(when we come out from among them that he will receive us).And that we will then be his sons and daughters.Yes, I imagine it takes something to totally separate yourself from the cares of a worldly person whom you are unequally yoked to in marriage and you are trying to make it work. But it can, if you and that person are willing. You can't make a person receive something.I have also heard some stories of how men got beautifully saved by their wives salvation.Know that it did not come without a dog fight from the devil and great sacrifice on the part of the saved wife.It can be done.I can do all things through Christ that strengthens me.We have talked about the unbelieving husband. Now let's talk about those that believe in God,but just won't except their wives as ministers.What?Did the word of God come out of your mouth?

One in the Spirit

The common equation of sin

1 Co. 14 v. 34 Let your women keep silence in the churches; for it is not permitted unto them to speak;but they are commanded to be under obedience,as also saith the law.Here Paul is telling the men about their wives speaking in the church.Verse 35 And if they will learn anything, let them ask their husbands at home; for it is a shame for women to speak in the church.Talking about their running mouths disrespecting the holyghost.Look at the very next verse of scripture and what Paul says next.Verse 36 What? Came the word of God out from you?Or came it unto you too? It is not really the clearest of understanding,but it seems as if paul is asking about the word of God coming from someone unexpected or some woman unexpectedly.And it also sounds as if he is asking someone else did they think that God was only speaking to them. All of this after he talked about it being a shame for a woman to speak in the church.He sounded rather surprized.We all come to a point in the spirit where things are not what we thought they were. That is what revelation is.The ministry that I mentioned in the beginning of this book, that I was in, where the woman thought she could insight a war in the church and the women were not being validated as ministers because the men were under this kind of teaching. They were being taught that women were suppose to be in subjection at home and of coarse;the women were too.There was also a hidden agenda in the teaching that women could not preach like the men. Also that women were not prophets or apostles. They could teach, but only at certain times and seasons.Not on a regular basis.My husband thought that I had a strong gift of discernment.He did not fully except the fact that I was

called as a prophetess.This type of teaching challenges the manhood of the men.It makes them feel as if they have to keep the women under control and if they don't, then they have failed as stewards of God's house.Some pastors allow this type of control on the male part because they don't want to do their jobs as a pastor by confronting a rebellious woman such as this sister.

One in the Spirit

Chapter 3

God's spirit is without limit

As I said my husband had a
hard time with the fact that I had a call as a prophetess.God
didn't really allow him to see it until after we were married.
Now I told him,but he thought it was cute and that I was a
person with dead on discernment. This word that we were
being taught was also constricting and limiting to the women
as I said earlier.The women that had no problems with this
type of teaching had identity problems and some had no idea
what it was they were called to do.Some never even sought
the Lord about a gift or a calling.So they thought the women
that had a call were trying to be rebellious like this sister.This
doctrine was being taught in another ministry where it seemed
to be working. You have to understand that the teaching I am
speaking of is a teaching that took submission to a whole new
level.I was being told even though my gift was accurate that
I had to check with my husband before I said anything in the
church.Like I said, we are not always in the spirit.My husbands
mind may have been on a Bulls game. How was he to know
what the spirit was giving me all the time? God dealt with my
husband and he accepted the fact that I had a sure calling
of God on my life.The leadership had meetings to even set
me down,but God kept confirming the call on my life through
complete strangers.Evangelist and visiting prophets as guest
speakers in the church who knew nothing of the situation in
the ministry, unless God revealed it to them.The pastor even
went so far as to tell my husband to set me down.My husband
replied",you're the pastor;you set her down.I didn't call her and
I won't set her down".When a pastor doesn't want to confront

a person and uses others to do their assignment as a pastor it causes a spirit of lawlessness. The pastor in my case said he didn't want to set me down because he felt as though the holyghost was giving me certain confirmed messages that was accurate and he didn't want to stop or quench it. Yet, he would ask my husband to do the dirty work for him. Pastors have to stand for something or fall for anything. They should obey the spirit of God in cases such as mine and this sisters. One of us was right and one wrongly being used by a bad spirit of confusion. Both, the sister and I should have been judged by the word of God and not gender.

One in the Spirit

God's spirit is without limit

This binding type of teaching makes women feel that their role in ministry is limited,if at all.To give you more of an idea of what type of confusion it brought.We had people,male and female literally wrestling over who got the microphone to speak.A time limit was put on women who were aiiowed to speak of about two to five minutes.Men were given more time to say what it was that they felt God gave them.There were men put in position that wasn't living holy at all.They still had addictions and habits and shouldn't have been given those positions.Women who were anointed were kept on the back burner,so it wouldn't make the men who were not anointed look bad.When the older woman I told you about earlier asked why did the women have to be set down in one meeting we had in particular.The pastor said ",so the men could step up and do what it was they were suppose to do".That never happened.My husband was one of the few anointed men in the church;with an anointed message on the end time and end time events.He was being put on the spot to enforce a lot of the pastors dirty work;which most of the time, he refused.The pastor had another church to see about as I said,so a lot of his time was spent there.The spirit behind this stuff promoted a gap in the church between the male ministers and the female ones. Not to mention the problems it brought in marriages.Some people ended up divorced because of the bondage teachings.Some could not stand under the pressure.We had friends that left the church far ahead of us being booted out after the devil took over. One man, that was a prophet said that God told him to get his wife out or it would destroy her.Emotionally, the damage was heart wrenching. It is the little foxes that spoil the vine, as Jesus said. Little things we think that don't matter. Prophet after prophet came through that church and warned the people that God said ;touch not my anointed and do my prophet no harm. Their was a lot of confusion and conflict. To tell the truth,we had people that walked all over the pastor and women who were anointed of God, that didn't live to even tell about it. There was a lot of deaths as a result of there disobedience to what God was saying and their grieving of his spirit.Nu. 23 v. 19 God is not a man, that he should lie;neither the son of man,that he should repent;hath he said,and shall he not do it?Or hath he spoken,and shall he not make it good?

One in the Spirit

God's spirit is without limit

God's spirit is without limit. Or so we have heard. I have heard so many great evangelists say this,yet it took years for some of them to allow their wives to come forth because of ignorance,fear of the opinion of others,or pure non acceptance. Either way it shouldn't have been.Some say, "well,it's because our children were young and she had to stay with them".It never stopped me.I just set my schedule at the right time and season. I would preach more during the summer when my children were out of school and let's face it;she didn't make those kids by herself. There were times when I really didn't want to leave my children,but I had to, for the sake of the call.It was a great sacrifice.My bible tells me it is better to obey than to sacrifice,so I figured the reward of obedience was greater than what had to be sacrificed. Let's make clear that I am not saying that every woman has been called to preach.I do believe that every person;male or female has a call to something for God.I am not so hung up on women answering the calls on their lives where I will say all are called.St. Mt. 20 v. 16 So the last shall be first,and the first last; for many be called,but few chosen. Every woman has not been chosen for ministry;just as every man has not been chosen for particular things.Some of the men in the ministry I told you about were not spiritually qualified to do the work that they were assigned.I have been in services and heard sisters, so called, preaching or teaching and it was like bad theater. Brothers too!It was like going to a show that you thought was worth seeing and finding out after the first act that it was a wash.I have been in services so bad that my spirit would get grieved and I would leave because of the vexation of it all.

My husband,being the gentlemen that he is,would sit through the torture and endure, in order not to be rude.You know the kind of services where everybody is kind of feeling their way. Groping like blind men as Jesus said.The bible says let all things be done decently and in order.I know we all have to start somewhere. Thats not what I'm talking about.I mean twenty years and you still don't have a clue?

One in the Spirit

God's spirit is without limit

So we are not saying that everybody has been called to be great evangelists in the kingdom. Some pastors wives are lousy co-pastors and they need to be somewhere knitting or cooking if it suites them.This is another type of bondage.These women are told that they are the co-pastor of a work because God has put their spouse in the position of pastor and this is what God is expecting them to do.This puts pressure on a woman to perform in another setting,because now she has to prove she is called.St. John 1 v. 12 But as many as received him,to them gave he power to become the sons of God,even to them that believe on his name;13 Which were born,not of blood,nor of the will of the flesh,nor of the will of man,but of God.Some preach because their mommas told them they should. Some preach because their friend Suzy does it.So how come I can't?

Others preach because they put enough money in the church to say what they want, when they want.It is a popularity contest to some.I met a lady recently who was invited to do a women's day program at a church because she could sing and the pastors wife was her aunt.She is not living a saved life and is in a fornication relationship with a man she hardly knows. There are people I know personally, who invite women to their church for the same reason men do.You scratch my back and I'll scratch yours.Politics in the church.And we wonder why real anointed vessels are hindered in ministry and not being used. The people are left confused and end up believing lies.Some of those people in the church I keep referring to went to their graves not believing women could preach.These errors have to be exposed in the church or we will continue to miss out on great blessings that the Lord has for all of us.The pastor in the church that fell apart, I believed had a problem with women anyway,because of his own personal issues with his personal life, ordained his wife as a co-pastor years later;unqualified of coarse.

One in the Spirit

God's spirit is without limit

Yes, he ordained her years later after telling me, without apology,that women just was not called as pastors.And this was because they had joined a denomination that believed in women and ministry,including female pastors and he couldn't look bad.So it is never too late to change for whatever your motive might be.The task before us all as Dr. Miles Monroe so intelligently and anointedly put it is to find our purpose.I would be in error myself if I leave purpose out of this book.Without that we are altogether lost. It is the key to who we are in life and in God.Most women are not taught to find purpose.They are told that this is what women do.So they try their best to emulate what they are even shown in some cases to do. I tell young girls all the time that they are more valuable than any designers original.That they are the designers original,wonderfully and fearfully made in the image of God.When we think this way it frees us to be an original and not try to be like someone else.Pray,teach and preach like you;the original and authentic you.When we rely on the spirit of the Lord it empowers us to do more than what we thought we could.Especially when you know that you have been called and qualified.Why is qualification so important in ministry?Ro. 8 v. 30 Moreover whom he did predestinate, them he also called,them he also justified;and whom he justified,them he also glorified.I told you earlier that there were some women that I knew that said they felt the call they had belonged to a man.Why would the bible talk about predestination.Predestination=the act of foreordaining to an earthly lot or eternal destiny by devine decree;also;the state of being so foreordained.To settle beforehand.God had to know exactly what he was doing when he called some. Unfortunately,some peoples hearing is off.He neither called, nor predestined them to do some of the stuff they say he did.It is the reason people make a mockery out of the church.There is a well known lesbian comic who was seen acting as though she was laying hands on people and they were falling down as if the power of God hit them.The power of God should have hit everyone of them for real,so they could get delivered.The point is that when we can't make it;we fake it in church and it shouldn't be.

One in the Spirit

God's spirit is without limit

Ro. 8 v 30 talks about justification. God will always back his word.This is why I believe through prayer and supplications these hindering forces have come to a place of exposure.The bible says that what is done in the dark will be exposed in the light.God's word is sure and he will not allow it to fall to the ground.This is why we have prophetesses like Juanita Bynum on the scene in this last hour of the church, to tell the truth and shame the devil.An awesome price has to be paid to walk in the level of anointing that she walks in.She has made history in the end time church because of her boldness and the fact that she is willing to expose herself as a willing vessel under the hand of God.I am an admirer of hers and use to watch on local television in Chicago years ago.The Lord has raised this woman to unbelievable heights in ministry and we have seen nothing yet. Paula White is another true vessel of God,raised up with an endtime message to bless the church.And I will not fail to mention Joyce Myers, a soldier as Debra in the last day church to get the troops ready for war.These are a few of the champions God has raised in order to show the devil and his people that when it comes to the ministry,gender is not a factor. Yet,we are still slow to accept the facts.Through pompous arrogance many of us,male and female, want to hold down or block anointed women in ministry.Nu. 23 v. 19 . . . ;hath he said, and shall he not do it?God is the author and finisher of our faith.We must begin a faith elevation so we can walk in the things he has called us to. When we allow our faith to rise through bathing it in prayer,fasting and the word, we will rise to the place of our destiny.God will perform what he said,but he is trying to find that virtuous woman he can illuminate with his power and glory. As Joseph we must first know our enemy.

One in the Spirit

God's spirit is without limit

Know your enemies. Sometimes we don't understand that the sister we think is a friend is one of the biggest, if not the biggest enemies that we may have. Anyone draining you everytime you go around them and not complimenting the anointing on your life is a leach. There are some women who as some men;that would rather you not go forward than to celebrate your calling with you.If you are not careful the devil will sneak up on you unaware.I once had a lady that was in my life for fifteen years who I thought was a friend.She always had something negative to say about any given situation.No matter how the spirit of the Lord would move,a complaint was always in her mouth. We had a move of God in the city of Chicago and a lot of people were touched, healed and delivered.Some had not experienced a move of God in years.All she wanted to know was how come I had to sing the same song so many times.I found myself explaining to her that there was a lady in the services that needed a miracle and that she needed to hear the song(healing Jesus) and get it in her spirit.I shouldn't have had to explain my actions to her,but this is the type of person she is.Another time we were at one of my mentors church in the same city and there was a spirit of witchcraft at work in the ministry. The Lord had me to open the doors in the back of the church and send the demons out.I don't know why God has to do things certain ways at certain times. He just does. The pastor didn't have a problem with it and the problems that they were having in the ministry was confirmed by him.He later reported that the problems were not happening anymore. That wasn't good enough for her.She got in the car with me after the service and chewed me out about doing something strange and that the pastor was just being nice.She found out that the church was helped when the devil was exposed and stopped talking to the pastor and his wife,whom she knew for many years. I don't associate with her anymore,though I still love and pray for her.Jesus said love your enemies.Love your enemies, but know your enemies.

One in the Spirit

God's spirit is without limit

Before we go any further we must understand that knowing the enemy goes deeper than flesh and blood.Ephes.6 V 12 For we wrestle not against flesh and blood,but against principalities, against powers,against the rulers of the darkness of this world,against spiritual wickedness in high places.So our battle is not with people,brot hers,sisters,wives,husbands,friend or foe.Our battle is deeper than the flesh;it is in the spirit.So know that as the word of God states, satan is the accuser of the brethren.He is the one that is using the particular individual that you may be getting drained or hindered by.And we need not be shaken by it.It is his job to steal, kill and destroy by any means necessary. Your job is to determine that if it is for you to remain in a relationship with a person who does such things and will they ever come to a place where they will repent. The proper or biblical name for such a spirit of control is the spirit of Jezebel. Rev. 2 v. 19 I know thy works,and charity,and service,and faith,and thy patience;and thy works;and the last to be more than the first. 20 Notwithstandind I have a few things against thee,because thou sufferest that woman Jezebel,which calleth herself a prophetess,to teach and to seduce my servants to commit fornication,and to eat things sacrificed unto idols.21 And I gave her space to repent of her fornication ;and she repented not.The spirit of Jezebel that is being talked about here in Rev. 2,is not talking about a gender but a spirit that was allowed to control the servants of God and never,though given a chance,would repent.The spirit of Jezebel is the same mindset as the person of Jezebel and it is not specifically one gender.This spirit is a block and a disrtaction to the move of

God and the anointing of God.It perverts judgement or sound doctrine.Some are so carnal minded that they hinder women in ministry by using this spirit and even comparing it to a woman given authority from God.Thank God nothing can replace the true anointing of God.

One in the Spirit

God's spirit is without limit

To understand the operation of this spirit,the Lord allows us through the woman Jezebel to see how this munipulative spirit works.And remember,this spirit operates under a false anointing. It is the spirit that tries to make it look as if women should not be in a position of authority in the church.Let's look at how she operated in 1K. 21 ;She was upset at the fact that Nabal would not sell a field to her husband Ahab,so she had the man stoned to death.She wrote letters in her husbands name to all of the nobles and the elders in her husbands name and sealed them with his seal.I K.21 v. 11 And the men of his city,even the elders and the nobles who were the inhabitants in his city,did as Jezebel had sent unto them,and as it was written in the letters which she had sent unto them.By using her husbands seal which was the seal of the kingdom and its king,she knew automatically that all of the men that she wrote to would respond. She wrote those letters under a false authority that did not belong to her. She used two men labeled by the bible as the sons of belial to lie to the crowd when they falsely accused Nabal leading to his stoning and death.She was going to get what she wanted at all cost,even at the expense of a life.This spirit is strong enough to kill.This is why it's exposure is so crucial.It can tear up the work of God quicker than any spirit in a church.It's defining characteristic is it's need to control and lack of submission of any kind.It has the ability to show a false submission,but will soon raise it's controlling head to annihilate anything that opposes or resist what it wants and it will lie.It is a lying spirit and the person possessing it will lie to you.

One in the Spirit

God's spirit is without limit

I will use as an example a situation where we were in ministry with a man who had the calling of a prophet. First glance at this person and the ministry he had, you would think that all was well.He was a faithful member of church and gave into the ministry tremendously to help with every cause.He had a beautiful gift of prophesy,but something was fishy.The longer he stayed around the ministry,the more his secret began to be revealed.He came to the ministry by a mutual contact who swore he was the best thing since sliced bread.As the months began to role along he got closer and closer to me and my husband.He came under the impression that he would be groomed for a higher place in ministry while supporting the work that we had begun.It wasn't even six months before the Lord had revealed to me that he had a strong spirit of homosexuality.This Jezebel spirit had been in operation all along.He came in under the pretence of being some great help in the ministry and he was.He also operated in a powerful anointing.The tell,tell signs were that he liked to be with the men more than women and an effeminant spirit would show up when he became most comfortable with people.He had a fiance to cover his self and so that no one would notice what he was trying to hide.He would constantly give himself away by directly ignoring all established house rules if we were out of town.This person had been in ministry before I was.As a matter of fact he was in ministry when I got saved.I did wonder why he fled from where he had been in ministry so long.God revealed that not only was he at work in a false submission and false anointing when he wasn't yielded to the spirit,but so was the fiance. This woman knew my ministry was a ministry of deliverance and she sent him for a season and even pretended that she would later come to the ministry as the Lord was leading her.As I stated earlier,this spirit will destroy and eventually kill the presence of God's influence over the people.The Lord had shown me all that he was doing and he was exposed by the holyghost.He packed his bags and fled without taking all of his things.As quickly as he came, he left without a word.Thank God.

One in the Spirit

God's spirit is without limit

Remember now, how Jezebel behaved in 1 K 21. She was only helping her husband get what he wanted.She didn't care who got hurt in the process. We had a service one time and my husband and I were both out of town when this man was allowed to preach.He yelled at a young lady in the middle of worship and said that God didn't want anybody clapping their hands while worship was going on.This young lady was already struggling with some things and didn't need him to shake her up any more than she was.I corrected him and he just looked at me as if I was wrong for saying anything to him.There was a guest speaker on another occasion and specific things were written down for those left in charge to do.He took it upon himself to do exactly what he felt a spirit leading him to do and ended up offending the guest speaker and me.Jezebel was only helping the king get what he wanted in her eyes.She saw Nabal as an enemy to that cause,so she eliminated him.This brother was helping us also. He felt as though the Lord was leading him and it didn't matter what I, or anyone else had to say about it.He wasn't wrong;we were.Rev. 2 v 21 And I gave her space to repent of her fornication;and she repented not.God will always give us space to repent.What does this have to do with women and ministry?This spirit is more subtle on women and it as earlier stated,makes it more difficult for a woman operating in a true anointing to go forward when a hostile environment has been created by another woman who has been used by this spirit.People tend to be more skeptical and less yielding when they have been overtaken in error.This is why the pastor has to be on cue.He or she has to possess the ability to drive the wolf.When there is a wolf among the sheep it has to be exsposed to the congregation or some will fall for this spirit unknowingly.The word coming across that podium has to be strong enough to reveal this demon.If not the ministry will suffer loss and quality ministry will suffer the lack of attention needed to destroy yolks.The people have to focus on the real and break off from what is false.

One in the Spirit

God's spirit is without limit

Why is this spirit harder to detect in women? Because we are the weaker vessel.That is not a bad thing.It was meant by God for good and satan always wants to pervert that which was meant for good.1 Pe. 3 v 7 Likewise,ye husbands,dwell with them according to knowledge,giving honor unto the wife,as unto the weaker vessel,and as being heirs together of the grace of life;that your prayers be not hindered.This scripture is not talking about a physically weak vessel.It is talking about a woman being emotionally weaker than a man.There are some women who are stronger than men,especially female athletes.This is why the men are being told of what their ministry to their wives should be.Women are more sensitive than men because God made us that way.This spirit gets down in the emotions as most spirits of this nature do.It is paranoid and can make the person think that everybody's out to get them.It can cause the person possessing it to go from one extreme to the other. Now some mental illness is real and generational;this thing is different.Most of the time when a person is diagnosed as bipolar, it's not a bipolar disorder at all.It is this spirit trying to overtake their mindset and overtrhow rationing for reality or what is right.As I told you of the older woman in the previous chapter.She was even on some type of nerve pill for bad nerves.I believe if she had got the prayer she needed to pinpoint this demon she could have been set free, if she wanted it.The similarity of her and the young prophet I told you about was bizarre.They both would go from one extreme to the next emotionally and craved a lot of attention.Both were healthy,but something was always wrong with them physically.

This spirit plays with the mind of its possessor and those under it's influence creating an environment of much drama. We are not talking about p.m.s.This is more traumatic.P.m.s. Goes away;this spirit persist and is relentless.When it seems as though the person that has it has calmed down;they rise up with even more turmoil,causing hinderance in the church.

One in the Spirit

God's spirit is without limit

This spirit is the number one reason that there is confusion in women's ministry.Even a lot of women, as I pointed out earlier, are confused.It is the counterfeit of the real thing.And some use it and biblical scriptures, out of context to say that this spirit pertains only to women trying to do something they were not called to do.Through revelation and in the book of revelations, we can see that this spirit is being talked about using not the old testament Jezebel,but people, male and female.Just as the bible talks about the spirit of Elisha;so it speaks of the spirit of Jezebel using people.Comparing this type of spirit to the spirit of the living God is equivalent to comparing night and day.One brings life to the body of Christ and the other breads death to all who accept it.Jezebel was nothing like the proverbs 31 woman,she was a rebellious manipulator. She was cocky and boisterous and good at fighting battles that didn't belong to her.Her children were rebellious and cursed.Her husband was lifeless, purposeless and really didn't have a clue as to how to be a man or a king.He had control over nothing when it came to his house, and had no idea of what his wife was up to on a daily basis.They had little communication and no real love for each other.Jezebel didn't do what she did out of love or loyalty.She did it out of contempt and spite; to show her false power and let her enemies know who the boss was. Her power exudes from the belly of hell itself.The proverbs 31 woman is a blessing to all who knows her.She shines from within. Wherever she goes she brings life.She blesses before she curses;gives before she takes and like Joseph her ministry is to preserve life,not to destroy it.Her purpose in life is to do the will of God.Her biggest service is to him; her strength comes from the Lord.It is refreshing to see her.When she is gone she is missed by those use to her company.She is a keeper. There is no limit to her because her faith and hope is in God's provision. Night and day is the difference between these two. Just as Kane and Abel the two are enemies;one much more deadlier than the plague.

One in the Spirit

God's spirit is without limit

It's no wonder that this generation is having so many marital problems because of the hindering of women in ministry and their husbands being confused to their own personal roles.Let's look back again at this virtuous woman in proverbs.Pr. 31 v 11 The heart of her husband doth safely trust in her,so that he shall have no need of spoil.11 She will do him good and not evil all the days of her life.The virtuous woman's man;if he is a God fearing man understands that there is more to her than meats the eye and if she is smart enough to care for him and his children,she is smart and anointed enough to hear from God.He knows that the Lord has more for his wife than just the family.She has a purpose in ministry also and he is strong enough to handle and respect that.This woman traveled to different parts of the land and elsewhere to bless their house and he didn't mind because it blessed him also. These things in today's society are taken lightly and sometimes are not appreciated.Woman's ministry is a dinosaur that's been unearthed time and time again. Look at a few bible facts.We were the last at the grave.Mk. 15 v 47 And Mary Magdalene and Mary the mother of Joses beheld where he was laid.The women were not afraid of the consequences of their fate.They loved the Lord and was in sorrow of his sacrifice for mankind of laying down his life.Mt. 28 v 8 And they departed quickly from the sepulchre with fear and great joy;and did run to bring his disciples word.These same women were the first to proclaim the resurrection.They were rejoicing and had great fear.That sounds like a good news message if I ever heard one.The first preacher to the Jews was a prophetess named Anna.Lu. 2 v 36 And there was one Anna,a prophetess,the daughter of Phanuel,of the tribe of Aser;she was of a great age,and had lived with an husband seven years from her virginity;37 And she was a widow of about fourscore and four years, which departed not from the temple,but served God with fastings and prayers night and day.38 And she coming in that instant gave thanks likewise unto the Lord,and spake of him to all them that looked for redemption in Jerusalem.

One in the Spirit

Chapter 4

The markings of a chosen vessel

We looked at the ministry of Anna, the daughter of Phanuel,a prophetess as the bible says in Lu. 2 v 36.She had all the markings of a chosen vessel.The first mark of ministry ordained by God is proof of a calling by use of gift.The second is life or the life of God coming out of that gift.The third mark is being willing to lay down your own way to find God's way.The forth is being a living sacrifice.Fifth service to others.Sixth a dedication to the time it takes to be made ready.The seventh and most important of all a life of fasting and much,much prayer.The first mark is found in 1 Ti. 1 v 6 Wherefore I put thee in remembrance that thou stir up the gift of God,which is in thee by the putting on of my hands.7 For God hath not given us the spirit of fear;but of power and of love and of a sound mind.The first mark of a chosen vessel is the responsibility to keep that which is trusted to them from the Lord.Paul is speaking to Timothy about what he has been given and the fact that he was not only given a gift but the power to stir that gift.It's like a car that has the ability to gas up on it's own.We can be renewed by faith;regenerated by the word of God anywhere and anytime we want or need it.The second mark ; the life of God coming out of our gift is found in 1st John 5 v 11 And this is the record that God hath given unto us eternal life,and this life is in his son.12 He that hath the Son hath life;and he that hath not the Son of God hath not life. Plainly the scripture is telling us that if we have or are walking in the anointing which is found only in Jesus Christ,we have life;eternal life.And this is the purposing of gifting.Not just to get people saved, but to give them something that will last forever,some thing that will sustain them in this life and help them make it to heaven. The third mark of laying down your own way to find God's way is in St. John 10 v 15 As the father knoweth me,even so know I the father; and I lay down my life for the sheep.Make no mistake;finding God's way is giving, giving and more giving,of you.You have to have something,to give something,or you will burn out.People make me ill trying to monopolize ministry.Making it out to be some type of glamourized sport.

One in the Spirit

The markings of a chosen vessel

Yes a glamour sport! We have a lot of people who look at ministry as if it is a vocation.Some type of career that they chose as a college major.It is a calling;a devine calling and should be looked at as such.We have preachers calling themselves motivational speakers?The bible does not say that in the last days there will be motivational speakers.It does not say that his lecturers will be flames of fire.We criticize each other and are gender biased,but we can't see the real danger of the denial of who we are and what we have been called to do.If people don't open the doors to you because of your calling; keep on praying,fasting and living. In the days ahead of this church they are going to need the genuine thing.You can't put V.W. Parts in a Mercedes. Nothing can replace the anointing ;nothing.So it is a joy to be in ministry,but not the kind of joy the world has.It is the joy of the Lord,which is our strength.We do not mourn as the world and we definitely don't rejoice as they do;yet there are some who try to mimic the joy the world has and that causes you to lose focus on the true joy of the Lord.Paul was beaten,suffered shipwreck,stoned and thought dead,jailed and had a thorn in his flesh and still stated for him to die was gain with Christ.We rejoice not at a concert when we get happy; but we rejoice at the work of the kingdom getting done and reaching the lost.A lot of women and men alike get in ministry for the wrong reasons. Some use the church to have an audience for a bigger plan of celebrity. The bible does not say that in the last days there will be movie star preachers.Be hot or cold, or God will spit you out.Out of the anointing, out of his presence,out of heaven.The real work of the kingdom is souls; not how good we preach, but who did we reach.St. Mt. 7 v 21 Not everyone that saith unto me,Lord,Lord,shall enter into the kingdom of heaven;but he that doeth the will of my father which is in heaven. This false wave of God that has entered the end time church is a catalyst to spark one of the greatest moves the church will ever see.Yes the false anointing that some can't tell the difference in is here.All this celebrity in the church and millionaire status being more important than getting your heart right with God.Money may come,but it won't by you out of hell. Ask the rich man who wouldn't feed Lazarus.

One in the Spirit

The markings of a chosen vessel

We do need to spend more time on this subject.Since we are talking about chosen vessels. Sanctification means being set apart.Sanctify= to make holy;consecrate;to free from sin.You can go to the sinner and not be a part of the sin.I heard a preacher say on world wide television that we better let people kind of do what they need to do, as in continue in their sin or we will lose them.We don't catch them. So how can we lose them?If we let God catch them through the anointing ;we can never lose them ;even if we never see them again. There are gospel singers that are trying to be super models and they say they are sold out to God.Preachers trying to become celebrities starring in plays where everything goes on in.I saw a movie a preacher made and it had just as much violence in it as any movie on t.v. And included a rape scene without warning.Trying to be like the world. Ja. 4 v 4 Ye adulterers and adultresses,know ye not that the friendship of the world is enmity with God?Whosoever therefore will be a friend of the world is the enemy of God.I heard a well known gospel singer say that just because she is friends with well known rappers, people give her a lot of flack, and so they should.Some preachers brag on how many celebrities they have in their church,instead of how much anointing. Paul said I boast in Christ.How much anointing do you have in your church.This is a celebrity type of anointing;pushing a politically correct doctrine that says you can stay in your sin and still be saved.Some who use to take a stand say they are now preaching a friendlier gospel that doesn't scare people,but shows the love of God and the compassion of Christ.God is love as the bible states;but if you love someone you will tell them the truth.Thy word is truth.St. John 17 v 17 Sanctify them through thy truth;thy word is truth.

One in the Spirit

The markings of a chosen vessel

This subject is very touchy and hush,hush,among preachers who want to keep their good standing with their friends. Saved friends and unsaved friends.I know we have to live in this world and have to live with people who may not ever accept Christ.This is to be expected.I also know that we have to do business with them, be friendly and more important,love them;we have to witness and tell them about Jesus.I just don't feel that we have to put on a falseness in order to reach in and get someone else out.For instance, I can't rap,so I'm not going to try.It is stupid to see someone over the hill trying to win young children by rapping.Some do and that's o.k., If you do.However, if it don't fit;you must quit.We are not fooling young people and this is another reason why God is raising up women who know that he has various callings, know their role in ministry and know who is to do what.They understand that they have to have their heads covered to take these churches to the next level and have a covering anointing to nurture and protect the ministry.And it is supported by the following scripture;1 Co. 11 v 5 But every woman that prayeth or prophesieth with her head uncovered dishonoureth her head;for that is even all one as if she were shaven.6 For if the woman be not covered, let her also be shorn;but if it be a shame for a woman to be shorn or shaven,let her be covered.7 For a man indeed ought not to cover his head,for as much as he is the image and glory of God;but the woman is the glory of the man. 8 For the man is not of the woman;but the woman of the man.9 Neither was the man created for the woman;but the woman for the man.10 For this cause ought the woman to have power on her head because of the angels.11 Nevertheless neither is the man without the woman,neither the woman without the man,in the Lord. The woman in ministry needs to understand that she has to be covered or crash.She has to have the support of her husband and be spiritually covered. In some cases her husband is not in a place to cover her spiritually ;but he can support her morally.If there is outside covering for the ministry with the approval of her husband it's o.k. As long as she is covered.

One in the Spirit

The markings of a chosen vessel

Women uncovered can't fight off the enemy alone, We must have pastoral covering,even as pastors.My covering is my husband,Apostle Dixon.It is difficult at times and his job is not the easiest.I have to know when it is my pastor talking to me and when it is my husband talking.He has to know when he is correcting his wife and when he is correcting the pastor.God set up our ministry this way and praise God ;it works.It is still a reproach to go forward in ministry without a covering.Someone who you will be accountable to who is able to tell you the truth and rebuke you in love.And when that person happens to be as close to you as a spouse,through trial and error, you learn to listen. There are some matters as a pastor that I don't touch without counsel.

In some cases I know just what to do.When it is something that I feel I don't have clear understanding on I ask questions. That is what a covering is for.A spiritual covering also has to know you as a person and in the spirit.The bible says to know no man after the flesh,but it also says to know those that labour among you.The person covers you in prayer and fasting.They are a shield against the attacks of satan. One can put a thousand to fleight.Two can put ten thousand to fleight. It is a discredit and a disgrace to not have someone to protect the anointing on your life and to correct you when you are wrong.There was a sister in one particular city,who God used me and my husband to raise up as a pastor.She called us and asked us to pray with her because she was being called to pastor.We didn't pay attention again to the signs in front of our faces.First, she said that she believed that God was putting her underneath us as her covering.She said that she felt that she was suppose to work with us for a season.We agreed to work with her to train her.

One in the Spirit

The markings of a chosen vessel

After she came to a few of our crusades, we found she had some things that she was hiding from us.She knew that we were setting up a church in the city where she was and there where people that she had coming to her house for church meetings. We were moving in a level of deliverance she had never seen before and instead of bringing the people that she had her little personal meetings with,she came and got blessed herself.After we moved to the city to set up this work we found out about these people or they heard about us.She had no choice but to bring them to the meetings. The people began to get healed and delivered and she began to try to keep them back, as it was,from us.She soon said God was telling her to start her own work and that she would still be under the covering of our ministry.She didn't want to tithe at all;only give offerings as she so felt lead.She would use me to do revivals and build her church;while we were trying to set a work up in the same city.The problems started to escalate when pride began to swell her head like an oil drum.I kept trying to tell her that we were there for a season and that the work set up was for her to pastor,not me.She became a monster as she began to dictate under a powerful spirit of control and witchcraft.She would bark orders out at people and even told me one time that I could not preach about homosexuality because she was related to one of the two lesbians in the congregation.I was not about to compromise my message to make someone living in abomination comfortable and I didn't.This only enraged her more, when the two stormed out. Nobody ever told her what or how to preach.The straw that broke the camel's back was when a young lady told her she wanted to leave her church and follow us. She calmly told the young lady she would release her and got right on the phone and rebuked me.She said I should have made her stay. We do not own people;they are not cattle or pets.They have there own mind, wills and emotions.You know the rest;she snapped and from what I hear is still snap, crackling, and popping.We found out from others that she was repreaching every sermon she heard me preach.And what is really sad is the fact that God was trying to raise her up to pastor the work we started. She kept harrassing me and told me she called every pastor she knew to discredit me in that city.I still pray for her.

One in the Spirit

The markings of a chosen vessel

The forth mark of a chosen vessel is being a living sacrifice.There was a great female pastor that lived in the city of Chicago,IL.,by the name of E.R. Alan.She was a prophetess like no other and highly used of God.She died at a young age of complications from an illness.The last thing I heard her say to God's people is that the Lord had given her this scripture to them, if they didn't remember anything else.Ro. 12 v 1 I beseech you therefore, brethren, by the mercies of God, that ye present your bodies a living sacrifice,holy,acceptable unto God, which is your reasonable service. Sacrifice= The offering of something precious to diety.2 Something offered in sacrifice.3 Loss,deprivation.4 To accept the loss or destruction of for an end,cause,or ideal.This is not a glamourous life;something has to be given and something has to be surrendered for a greater cause. It is no street called easy.It is a street called straight.The grand prize is our eternal reward and Jesus Christ saying well done thou good and faithful servant.Serving a pure God from a pure heart.There are some still waiting for deliverance in some areas but they are presenting such as they have unto God.And these are the ones ;the Peters not yet converted.These are the underdogs that are the church of the eleventh hour waiting on that fire within to grow and consume everything that's not like God in order to be meat for the masters use.Those yet striving because they know they are still on a journey.Ph. 3 v 14 I press toward the mark for the prize of the high calling of God in Christ Jesus.It is still a pressing way.The bar remains high,no matter how far we have come. And this too,is to keep us humble.Just in case we think we have arrived. The last arrival will be heaven or hell and no stops in between.

One in the Spirit

The markings of a chosen vessel

Press=Tobeardownupon;push steadily against. 2 Assail,compel.3 To squeeze out the juice or contents of.4 To squeeze to a desired density,shape, or smoothness.5 To try hard to persuade;urge.6 To follow through;prosecute.7 Crowd.8 To force ones way.9 To require haste or speed in action.This is what it meant when we heard the old church mothers tell us." Child,it's a pressing way".The way of ministry and having a life of spiritual success is different than the success that is worldly.Paul is using the comparison of pressing to express the hardship we have to sometimes face.I heard a successful preacher say ; "I have not suffered to get the anointing".In the next breath he told how he went through a sleeping disorder from wearing his self down from ministry. But he said he didn't know what suffering was.Maybe someone can look up what suffering means for him.There is some price he has paid to have the healing anointing that he has.It is not free;it costs a price to be a soldier for God.2nd Ti. 2 v 3 Thou therefore endure hardness, as a good soldier of Jesus Christ.4 No man that warreth entangeleth himself with the affairs of this life;that he may please him who hath chosen him to be a soldier.I remember a time when there was a move of God happening in our church and some of the young ladies there,who I knew well,where jealous of the successfulness of the ministry.The signs and miracles were so strong and the power of God was so miraculous they could not explain it.They began to look for things to tear down the reputation of the ministry.All of this started out of jealousy and because as with the older woman in the earlier chapters,they could not control the ministry or me.A seed of discord was sewn.Pr. 6 v 12 A naughty person,a wicked man,walketh with a froward mouth.13 He winketh with his eyes,he speaketh with his feet,he teacheth with his fingers;14 Frowardness is in his heart,he deviseth mischief continually;he soweth discord. The (disgruntled bunch);every church has them.They are just tools the Lord uses to keep you sharp.There was a time, when with this group, I would get mad because someone would call me a witch.I learned to let the anointing speak for me.

One in the Spirit

The markings of a chosen vessel

The fifth mark of a chosen vessel is your service to others.Service= The occupation of a servant.2 Help,benefit.3 The act,fact, or means of serving.4 Performance of official or professional duties.5 Serve.Ju. 4 v. 4 And Deborah, a prophetess,the wife of Lapidoth,she judged Isreal at that time.5 And she dwelt under the palm tree of Deborah between Rama and Bethel in mount Ephraim; and the children of Israel came up to her for Judgment. Judgment= A decision or opinion given after judging.2 The process of forming an opinion by discerning and comparing.3 The capacity for judging; discernment.Deborah was put in the book of Judges because she was a judge.She was chosen by God to set the children of Israel in order. As the scripture says she judged the people.When matters came up amongst the people the prophets would discern the matter and take things before God.Deborah didn't set under the palm tree to be cool, as someone I new put it.That place in the mountains was her high place for seeking God.She wasn't under the palm tree just for shade. That was her place of visitation and revelation from God.We all who are in service need a high place, away from everything else,so we can hear from the Lord.A private place that is not so private where we can't serve his people.You will notice the bible calls the tree, the palm of Deborah.We have to spend that secret time in that secret place with God,as psalms 91 says, we need to dwell in that secret place.But when it is time to go to war we have to be ready to accept the challenge as Deborah did, and ride with the troops to battle.To serve is to prepare,and so many in ministry,are ill prepared.When you do not give God time in prayer and meditation,you are not prepared for battle.Yesterdays anointing was for yesterday. This is why the bible tells us to remember not the former things and to neither bring them to mind. Some are still running off of the charge they got from a former victory and are not able to attain,because they are trying to maintain.

One in the Spirit

The markings of a chosen vessel

No, there is no such thing as maintaining in Service to others. The world does it's best to maintain. They try to maintain their money, their health status, their power. They believe in maintaining. We have to focus on attaining. Attaining= Achieve, accomplish.2 To arrive at;reach. We have to get to a place that's higher than where we are, so we can do more than what we think we can. Only in Christ can we reach the unattainable. When we go higher we make the way for others to. Having an ear like Deborah ;sharp enough to do battle. Spiritual sharpness in your gift and the guts to take on challenges, with God's help. How powerful! How Awesome! To God be the glory! The sixth mark;a dedication to the time it takes to be made ready. I heard a preacher say; "It doesn't take God all day to do something". This is true, however, it may take you all day to be made ready to do it. You probably are asking what do I mean by a dedication to time? Two scriptures come to mind. Ro 12 v 6 Having then gifts differing according to the grace that is given to us, whether prophecy, let us prophecy according to the proportion of faith;7 Or ministry, let us waite on our ministering;or he that teacheth on teaching. There has to be a time of dedication or patience. We can do or say something out of season and mess things up. Do you believe that God wants us to get it right every time like any good father. He knows that we won't though, so that's why he gives us grace and second, third, fourth and fifth chance to get it right. Another scripture we need to look at on time dedication is;Ephes. 5 v 15 See then that ye walk circumspectly, not as fools, but as wise, 16 Redeeming the time, because the days are evil. Redeem= To ransom, free or rescue by paying a price.2 To free from the consequences of sin.3 To convert into something of value. 4 To make good(a promise)by performing;fulfill.5 To atone for. We have to make good in our time.Stop lying to everyone by saying you are praying and you know you are sleeping.Take some serious time with the holyghost.

One in the Spirit

The markings of a chosen vessel

The seventh and most important mark.A life of fasting and much,much prayer.Mt. 17 v 21 Howbeit this kind goeth not out but by prayer and fasting.We know the story of the man who brought his son to the disciples and they could not cast a demon out that made him throw his self in water and at times in fire.This demon would not leave or(this kind) of demon would not leave unless there was prayer and fasting.Fasting causes the belly to sleep so that the spirit man can become stronger.Our battle is a spiritual one and our spirit man is strengthened when we allow that which causes the natural man to live to weaken and that which causes the spirit man to increase strengthen.Paul said, for me to die is gain with Christ.What he was saying was, Christ, the anointing on the inside of him was getting stronger when his fleshly man got out of the way.The belly is the natural man's fuel tank.It keeps the natural body active and alert. The spirit man's fuel tank is located in our soul.The soul consist of our mind, will and emotions.The spirit man where the presence of God lives.1 Co. 3 v 16 Know ye not that ye are the temple of God,and that the Spirit of God dwelleth in you(lives in you).If the battle is in the spirit,the spirit has to do the battling.Fasting and praying amplifies the word of God on the inside of us.We become spiritual power forces when we let God arise on the inside of us this way.Some people don't believe that we still have to fast and pray,but they can walk around with problems and conditions,wearing bracelets that read ;what would Jesus do?I've had deliverance teams go in places prayed up and fasting and we've had moves of God from simply doing what

Jesus did by faith and watching God work.God needs room to work in our temple.Sometimes there are so many other things in the temple, God doesn't have enough space to move.

One in the Spirit

The markings of a chosen vessel

God can't move, because you won't move and allow him to.There are some who can't fast because of medical reasons. I'm not saying you will not enter heaven or be saved if you don't fast.We're talking about the life of a chosen vessel here.God has certain things that are a must for those who are willing to pay the price. One time me and my husband got accused of trying to be super saints. I told the lady that to me all saints were super.All I know is that the bible says that special miracles were wrought by the hands of Paul and that Peters shadow had healing in it.These things didn't happen by the luck of the draw.They happened because these men had a life of giving themselves to fasting and praying and to the ministry of the word. Fasting and praying are the perfect combination for a miracle by faith. They are like adding a laundry booster and a stain remover to your wash;something extra to remove the stain of sickness and sin. Fasting also keeps us humble because we are made to realize through it that power belongs to God and that we need his help.Fasting helps us live in the spirit.This is why when Jesus was tempted of the devil after fasting for forty days and forty nights he was not moved.St. Mt. 4 v 4 But he answered and said, It is written,man shall not live by bread alone,but by every word that proceedeth out of the mouth of God. Our life is in the spirit and praying and fasting enhances that. These two are the activating forces, by which we, through the help of God, change circumstances.Without them we have the word of God to help us in our ministry.Personally,I feel without them I would not have been able to weather some of the storms I've had to face.They have helped me to focus more on the things of the spirit and are confidence boosters to aide in tasks that normally I would hesitate at.I was trained in the spirit by a man of God when I got saved at the age of nineteen to believe that when you fast, you last.And when you pray you stay. They are sustainers in your spiritual and ministerial walk.

One in the Spirit

Chapter 5

The men who set us free

It is a true blessing from God when you are able to let your hair down,take off your shoes,with no make up,and just be. Be who you are and not someone's mother,or someone's wife.Just be.And this chapter of my book is for the men who let us be.There are times, when my husband, who is a very understanding man,has told the children to just go and find something to do because he knows I am tired and that I need that alone time to regroup in order for me to be the woman he married and not some irritating monster.The bible says, husbands dwell with them(your wives) according to knowledge. You have to have enough patience to learn to understand your wife, and it is the same on the part of the wife.But it takes a man of true understanding to accept his wife in a calling from God and adjust to some of the things that are not considered the normal, that comes with that call.Let's look at some noble princes among men in the bible who stood by their wives in the midst of trying circumstances.St. Mt.1 v 18 Now the birth of Jesus Christ was on this wise;when as his mother Mary was espoused to Joseph,before they came together,She was found with child of the holyghost. We see here in the word of God it says that before they had any sexual intercourse as husband and wife that Mary was pregnant. What could have been the number of things going through this mans mind;thinking he had married a virgin,and he did. But just imagine if it were you.What would you do?St. Mt. 1 v 19 Then Joseph her husband,being a just man,and not willing to make her a publick example,was minded to put her away privily.Joseph was such a good man that he was willing, even if she had cheated on him,to divorce her privately in order that she would not be stoned to death,which was the punishment for adultery.Verse 20 But while he thought on these things, behold,the angel of the Lord appeared unto him in a dream, saying, Joseph,thou son of David,fear not to take unto thee Mary thy wife;for that which is conceived in her is of the holyghost. Joseph had enough patience and understanding to at least sleep on the matter before he did something he would have later regreted.He feared God and didn't want anything to happen to her.

One in the Spirit

The men who set us free

Joseph is a prime example of loyalty and faith. Though the bible tells us so little about him,he is still a spiritual giant. He fathered our Lord Jesus Christ.Not once does it say he was not a good father.He accepted Jesus as his own and didn't treat him as anything less.He stuck to his vows to his wife and feared the Lord.His ministry of a husband and father was second to none.He trained Jesus to be a carpenter.No one else in this world can own that one.He is most noble because he let Mary be who God called her to be and didn't try to fix it. He let the will of God be.He understood that his family was like no other and that he had to watch over what God was cultivating in the garden that was his family.We hear all of these stories on Esther and the bible talks about how she was loved of the king and found grace and favor,but let's look at some reasons why she turned him on.Est. 2 v 15 Now when the turn of Esther,the daughter of Abihail the uncle of Mordecai,who had taken her for his daughter,was come to go in unto the king,she required nothing but what Hagai the king's chamberlain,the keeper of the women,appointed.And Esther obtained favor in the sight of all them that looked upon her.The king was turned on with the fact that Esther was a real woman.She didn't need a lot of make up or fake hair to be who she was.And if you read this story you will see the great lengths that the kings people went through to purify the skin and groom these women to be queen.It was very complicated to go through all of the preliminaries and get them ready.This did not change who she was and that was what the king saw. An inner beauty;a jewel of great price. A Woman born to be his queen,which is something that can't be taught; it just has to be put there by God.The king saw the quality that he looked for in a woman.Someone with the ability to make him feel like he was the king.The love he had for this woman saved a nation;it doesn't get any better than that.

One in the Spirit

The men who set us free

The men in today's society may not have kingdoms and they may not be the one to say they taught Jesus to be a carpenter,but they are our kings who let us be free in the spirit to do what it is we have been called to do.They are not worried about what their friends think.They have sacrificed because they believe the God that they serve has called and is using us.So I salute the known and uknown soldiers, who back their wives in some tough situations and circumstances.I am talking about a brother who is not afraid to change a pamper,wash dishes or buy intimate feminine products for his wife.He knows this makes him more of a man because he is into his woman and her needs being met are more important than his.He knows that if she's been called to ministry,her days are going to be a little more complicated and that she will be fighting forces that the ordinary woman would not,so he bathes her in his prayers and words of comfort.He knows that there will be times when he has to let go and trust that she is in God's hands ;whether she is at home or half way around the world.He knows the best way to protect her is in the spirit, through prayers of supplication when words are simply not enough.He also knows that she would lay her life down for him the same way so that he can fulfill his destiny also;so he is confident in his trust towards his wife.The virtuous woman's husband trust in her. 2nd K. 4 v 10 Let us make a little chamber,I pray thee,on the wall; and let us set for him there a bed,and a table,and a stool,and a candlestick;and it shall be,when he cometh to us,that he shall turn in thither.The Shunamite woman's husband had to really have a lot of confidence in the judgement of his wife.How many husbands do you know in old testament, new testament or now, that would feel it is alright to let a man move in the house where they live and provide him with some essentials at that husbands exspense. Even if some allowed it, they still might say, let the prophet get his own lamp.This man was ultimately blessed because he allowed a blessing to come into his house through his wife and even gained a son who death could not soon take.

One in the Spirit

The men who set us free

My mother often told me that a strong man is not a man who can't cry,but it is the man who can cry.Growing up in the city of Chicago IL.,you had to be tough,or thought of as week. The little girls really thought it was a sign of weakness to see a little boy crying.In our particular culture;we were taught that being hard or fierce was a great strength.Then I read in the bible after I got saved that Jesus wept.St. John 11 v 35 Jesus wept.36 Then said the Jews,behold how he loved him!A strong man is not afraid to weep over those whom he loves and Jesus is our example of pure,heartfelt, love.He was not afraid to show his emotions. Men are taught to suppress their feelings and not to tell you when something hurts them. The bible teaches us that the truth makes us free.A man who has been set free by the hand of God allows others that they love to be free. This is such an important factor in ministry.He is free to ward off unlawful attacks of the enemy by standing in his God given place of authority as a protector.Because his wife knows her best interest is what he is protecting,there is a greater release of the anointing for God to move in the marriage and in the ministry. There is no room for competition and jealousy in a marriage built on integrity and trust. A marriage where the head is God and his word makes the rules. We have had several different people try to compare the way God uses me and the way he uses my husband.If you don't have confidence in what you have been called to do;the enemy will get in your marriage and hinder the ministry and your life.There were times when we would discern people trying to make me seem more important than my husband and there were times when people would try to make me feel as though I was not as important as my husband.God called us to unity in 1995.He let us know that we had to be one.We have all heard stories of how some man had a great ministry and then the devil would use his wife to tear him down and ultimately hinder, or even destroy his ministry. But what about that man who through envy or jealousy would allow the devil to use him to hinder or destroy.This is a real problem that exist in the church and is often ignored.

One in the Spirit

The men who set us free

I have personally heard horror stories from female pastors and evangelists who say they went through unnecessary grief at the hand of their men being used by the devil.In one instance a lady told me that every time she had to go on a crusade her sickly husband would pretend to get very,very, sick.She said she use to give in to this demon,but that she would comfort him the best she could and leave him with caretakers and go on and obey God.She said she would gently tell him that he knew that he wasn't really as sick as he was pretending and that she was going to still leave and do God's work. She said, he jammed the door shut slamming it and grouched until she left.Good for her!You can't feel sorry for the devil.He is subtle and full of tricks and lies.Another lady was powerful in prophesy.She married the wrong guy. Every time they would go somewhere to minister, he would compete because he also had a prophetic call. He was intimidated by her because her gift was more accurate.It became a contest and they would end up arguing and fighting. She cracked under the pressure, backslid and gave up on the ministry. The demon that used him accomplished it's goal and she wants nothing to do with ministry.There are brothers who want to control the way God is using their wife,when they know that they didn't call her.If you didn't do the hiring, you can't do the firing.God anoints and appoints;so he knows what he wants to do and who he wants to do it in.So we see that, there still is a lot of confusion,although there is a great deal of teaching going on in the area of ministry,more needs to be learned. I told you earlier that the Lord told us we had to be one in 1995.I must say,it took us about eight years to fully understand what he meant. Am. 3 v. 3 Can two walk together, except they be agreed?God was talking to a rebellious Israel not walking in his ways.You can go along with something and still not agree with it.The problem,however is larger than that. The sin comes in when we are not honest with each other about our true feelings.There are some teachings that say we have to go along with everything our husbands say,or we are not submissive.What if we looked at it this way?What if we could agree to disagree?

One in the Spirit

The men who set us free

Am. 3 v. 3 Can two walk together, except they be agreed?I told you it took us about eight years to figure out what God was saying, when he said, my husband and I had to be one. First of all we have a lot in common,but just as much as we have in common we are just that much more different.We hear people all the time talking about compatibility. Compatible= Able to exist or act together harmoniously.2 con sonant,congenial,symphathetic.If compatibility is so important in marriage then why do we see people who seem like they have nothing in common happily married for years and on the other hand people that have everything in common divorced. Maybe it's something more than compatability.It's the power of agreement.My husband does not agree with everthing I say and I don't agree with Everything he says.We were really having a serious split on some issues that came up at one time in our marriage and a light bulb came on in my head.It was as plain a day,what God told us.We had to be one.I suggested to my husband that we start to be okay With not agreeing on everthing.To agree to have our own opinion about something, without the other person being mad about it.This stopped a lot of confusion and battling over nonsense.We still have issues with some things, but they are not so weighty now. We are not called by God to do the same thing,so what more was God saying.Through the revelation of this one serious disagreement we learned that I agree with his freedom to obey the Lord even when it doesn't make sense or I can't see it.He learned the same.We learned that we are not children and that forcing somebody to do something that they didn't want to do was robbing the person of their wholeness.We let each other be free to have an opinion that was different from the others.True agreement had a different meaning to us now. Now it meant coexisting with respect to each others feelings even if one had to give up their decision to go the way of the other,and being honest about our feelings.One decision sometimes with two different, honest feelings about it.And if the decision didn't work out,admitting the other party was right.This of coarse takes humility and time.

One in the Spirit

The men who set us free

The men who set us free are not just husbands they are spiritual leaders who know what the will of God is in this earth.They are willing to say that they know that women have had and have a key role in ministry and are not helpless when it comes to a move of God.They are our spiritual fathers who undergird us and encourage us to follow God.They are wise men who the Lord has given special insight into us. They know that God is no respecter of persons and that his spirit is liberal.They are the Mordecai's guiding Esther into her place of favor.They know that if we are in our rightful place that they too, will be sustained.They are the promoters that push us with no selfish motives as Boaz;Just as he went before Naomi's people,before he married Ruth. He wanted what was best for her, before his own feelings.He was willing to allow a woman he cared about deeply to marry someone else because of his noble character. He respected her when she came in unto him, lifted his skirt and slept at his feet.He had integrity and was willing to set her free. These men have more of a mentoring spirit that enhances the gifting that we have.They are not like others who abort our visions because we are the wrong gender.They help to validate who we are and whose we are.They are not afraid to lay their hands on and ordain women in ministry and giftings.They allow the spirit of the Lord to move the way he wants to. They are not bound by tradition or doctrine of men.These are men who are mature in the Lord and are not intimidated if it happens to be a woman laying hands on them.They make up for those of us who have lost ground in other situations, by encouraging us to run with the vision that God has given us.They are men like my father who always encouraged me to try as hard as the men to accomplish things.Even though he wasn't saved when he was younger, before he passed, he was one of my greatest motivators, giving me the thumbs up in spite of all of the odds, to preach the gospel of Jesus Christ.

One in the Spirit

Chapter 6

The birthing pains of ministry

I told in some of the earlier chapters of how I went through some changes in ministry.I am a firm believer that all that happens to us is for a making to be what God intends.Ministry being birthed out is an important process, because it also gives us a validation.This is why it is so important to hold on to your God given vision and it proves that your vision is from God.It is our seal of approval. 2nd Ti. 2 v. 19 Nevertheless the foundation standeth sure,having this seal, the Lord knoweth them that are his.And,let everyone that nameth the name of Christ depart from iniquity.We can't say that we are called of God and love the wages of sin.Surely we don't expect God to bless us and live any kind of life.The world and its ways are very enticing and it takes a made up mind to be sold out to Christ.We have had to turn down several offers that would have been a great blessing to us. The Lord had other plans for us.He sometimes allows you to be tested, for you to see where your heart is,he already knows.I have had several people put things in front of me to promote my ministry, or so they said.Their intentions may have been good,but that wasn't the way God had for me. It is hard to look at others take what looks like a blessing at the time and it looks as though the person is prospering from it.Although everything in you may want to burst, the spirit of the Lord is telling you, you can't have it or it's not for you,or it's not the time for what your looking at.Thus we have a birthing pain for a true ministry. Some people get there any way they can. By hook or crook, it doesn't matter,as long as they think they're getting where they should be in ministry;but their house isn't being built right.Mt.

7 v. 26 And everyone that heareth these sayings of mine,and doeth them not,shall be likened unto a foolish man, which built his house upon the sand;We can't afford to build on sand. We have to have what God gives us setting on the foundation of God. Everything that is built has a blue print and a foundation. With every vision or gifting there is a plan and foundation.We know that the plan has to come out of the spirit of God, so why do we allow the enemy to feed us lies and end up getting into things that's not in the plan.

One in the Spirit

The birthing pains of ministry

Another birthing pain is what I call the (Joseph syndrome),it is where you tell your vision in innocence to the wrong person.I told a couple of pastors of the plans that I dreamed of for ministry and when the enemy started to fight and God was allowing me to go through a time of testing;these two began to enforce what I had spoken about in their particular ministries and was even successful at it.My vision also bread jealousy from people that I thought was in my corner.We all have to go through the (Joseph syndrome), if our vision is from God. Your vision may not be to be second in command in Egypt.It may be traveling the world, in missions,or pastoring.Whatever it is,if it is from God, it will be fought.You will look like a person that does not know what they are talking about in the beginning stages of it.The ones you tell about it will know that there's some truth to it because they know that God has called you.But because they are unsure in themselves they will make your way hard. This is why it is critical to stay on the path that God has for you.The Lord will back up what he says and prove his word.Getting off track will only delay his plans further for your life.Sure Joseph's brothers hated him,but in the end they needed him to stay alive in famine. God will make your enemies your footstools.St. Mt. 22 v. 44 The Lord said unto my Lord,sit thou on my right hand,till I make thy enemies thy footstool.Footstool= A low stool to support the feet.The Lord is saying that he will make your enemies the stepping stone to boost you up to where you are trying to get. He is saying here,for you to stay in right standing with God by forgiving your enemies.Stay in a seated,relaxed position and don't rise up against your enemies;God will rise for you. For you to die is gain with Christ.It's just a birthing pain!

One in the Spirit

The birthing pains of ministry

One of the biggest birthing pains you will encounter is rejection from people you know and that think they know you in your family.St. Mt. 13 v. 57 And they were offended in him.But Jesus said unto them,A prophet is not without honour,save in his own country, and in his own house. That house can include a lot of people who knew you back then.We have to keep ourselves in constant remembrance, that these are the ones whom the Lord and the devil use to keep our feet on the ground.I had a brother in the Lord, who just passed in 2005.He would boo-hoo, all the time because as he put it;his mother would not respect him for being the man of God that he was called to be.I knew this brother about seventeen years and nothing would get him down more than the comments of his mother.This is something that in ministry, we must overcome.I know he loved his mother,but you don't love anyone or anything hard enough, where it causes you to lose focus on who you are in Christ.Jesus cut off everything that hindered his work.Yes, we are to honor mother and father, but nothing comes before God.St Mt. 12 v. 46 While he yet talked to the people,behold, his mother and his brethren stood without,desiring to speak with him. 47 Then one said unto him,behold,thy mother and thy brethren stand without,desiring to speak with thee.48 But he answered and said unto him that told him,who is my mother and my brethren?49 And he stretched forth his hand toward his disciples, and said,Behold my mother and my brethren!50 For whosoever shall do the will of my Father which is in heaven,the same is my brother,and sister,and mother.Jesus makes it plain for us, so the devil can't fool us.They wanted him to stop what he was doing for some carnal matter that had nothing to do with the kingdom work he was doing.And wanted him to come where they were. We have to stay where God puts us and not compromise by coming down to the level of others;even those who we are related to.

One in the Spirit

The birthing pains of ministry

We talked about in an earlier chapter, the importance of knowing your enemies.Well, it is also very,very, important to know who your friends are.We are not talking about mentors;people who don't mind kicking your behind when you need it;in the spirit of coarse. But someone to love you unconditionally.A real heart shattering birth pain of ministry is thinking you have a friend that you don't have. People are so deceiving,and have no shame.You just about have to use discernment with the ones you think you know. It is a really big hurt to put your trust in someone and find out that you have been betrayed by someone that you would never betray.A true friend however,can tell you the truth about something and you will hear them if you trust them. There is nothing new under the sun.People can change like a werewolf on you,before you know it.Ps. 41 v. 9 Yea, mine own familiar friend,in whom I trusted,which did eat of my bread,hath lifted up his heel against me.David is letting us know what a so called,friend can do to you.He described a heel being lifted up against him.In other words,this friend was trying to,or did kick his behind.The devil puts the stupidest notions in peoples heads and they can sometimes lose their minds and not realize what they are doing.Sometimes they do know what they are doing and will not repent.We can't take vengeance,it is one of the laws of the kingdom and David knew it. Look at what he went on to say. Ps. 41 v. 10 But thou,O Lord,be merciful unto me,and raise me up,that I may requite them.Requite= To make return for ;repay.2 To make retaliation for;Avenge.3 To make return to.David in reference, was saying,Lord help me to avenge myself according to the your ways in righteousness.It is very painful to be humiliated and done all manner of ways by people and have the word of God say you can't tell them off or get them back.It is easy to tell someone else not to do something or say something to an enemy that is not yours. But when the shoes are on your foot they can feel too tight. The devil knows who to use to push your buttons.This is why it is so important to keep a steady and dedicated prayer life.It will keep you humble.

One in the Spirit

The birthing pains of ministry

Le. 19 v. 18 Thou shalt not avenge, nor bear any grudge against the children of thy people, but thou shalt love thy neighbour as thyself;I am the Lord.Vengeance belongs to God.It is human nature to retaliate and there is a relief that comes to the carnal mind of a false satisfaction when we get angry.Our fleshly man fell in the garden in Adam and that is the nature of a man without God ; to take vengeance.It is the nature of the beast;satan.Ec. 3 v. 21 Who knoweth the spirit of man that goeth upward,and the spirit of the beast that goeth downward to the earth?The fleshly man is the spirit of the beast.The spirit of the natural man;man without God. This nature kills,steals and destroys ;it is corrupt and it can hinder; literally taking years off of your life.We have to change the way we think or perish.The spirit of the man that goeth upward is the soul of a man full of the spirit of God. People perish for lack of knowledge.People perish for not thinking like Jesus.1st. Co. 2 v. 16 For who hath known the mind of the Lord,that he may instruct him?But we have the mind of Christ.We have the characteristics or ways of the anointed one or Christ.The way of Christ and this is our way of escape from the evil nature of this world, death and hell.The pain of not being or doing like others is a hard one, because in it we are challenged to be more like Jesus and this is one of the greatest test of a sold out,surrendered life.When I was younger in ministry,I thought that because I had a prophetic call I could tell people off. This stronghold of the mind came from others with prophetic calls.I thought it was o.k., to tell people what I wanted them to know when I wanted them to know it.I got a sense of a false satisfaction from this.Anyone that goes off(in the name of Jesus) and they are using a prophetic gift for snapping is lying if they say there isn't a release in this.The other thing is, it only last for a little while.If you really love God, you will feel really terrible afterwards and wish you hadn't said anything to the person and just prayed.I learned the hard way to stay back and pray.I am not saying I am one hundred percent delivered,I still have issues;but I am seventy five percent sure that my temper won't get me so worked up that I can't think straight. You can be angry and not sin.

One in the Spirit

The birthing pains of ministry

Bad behavior patterns or learned behavior is is what we are talking about.As a young pastor I did some things that I assumed was working for others and all it did was cause problems in the congregation with different individuals.We are not going to please everybody all the time ;but there are certain things we can do that may look as if it is working for someone else and it may not work for you.I thought what worked in other places would work where I was.I saw and experienced pastors slaving the people like task masters. I saw pastors that pimped the congregation like hirelings and think that it was o.k.I still know of some pastors who wear the people out and come up with some excuse as to condone their behavior.These things unfortunately are teachings from some of our fathers.You see, in some parts of the church it was considered all right to keep the pastors as poor as possible.That would keep them humble and the poorer they were kept,the holier they were.The extreme side of this was the vengeance of the pastors who were hirelings;deciding that they were not going to be the victim, but the aggressor.So they decided to go overboard and tax the people beyond limits.These are pimps and some of them are female.This pimp mentality is some of the reason why over seventy five percent of the church won't tithe.And some won't pay all of their tithe,because they feel as though they are being robbed and don't understand that they should tithe anyway and God will honor their giving by faith.I had a spirit of control that would pop up,because I would see other pastors do it and think it was the right way.There is a difference in control and order.Order brings unity and control brings strife.I learned to tell people what the Lord says and sleep at night. Yes, I would sat up at night worrying that someone didn't listen to my counsel. And would nag the person to try to get them to change.This spirit is overbearing. God said he would not strive always with man and I don't believe he wants us to.It is a given that there will always be goat among the sheep.When we realize the difference it gives us peace. We know who to give responsibility to and who not to.

One in the Spirit

The birthing pains of ministry

The birthing pains of pastoring, especially for a woman are different from any others in ministry. The pastor is married to the church;so that means in sickness and in health.A healthy church has to be balanced on all sides. It has to have it's candle wick trimmed. The bible gives us a good understanding about having our wicks trimmed and not letting our oil run out.We have to know that the kingdom of God, like any other has to be made up of it's people.St. Mt. 25 v. 1 Then shall the kingdom of God be likened unto ten virgins,which took their lamps, and went forth to meet the bridegroom.Ten is the number of power and it expresses the full potential of the power of God.In the world they have an expression of calling people who are very attractive "10's",this means they are more than the average beautiful;that there is some extra attribute that this person has that makes them stand out or outstanding.In the realm of the spirit ten represents explosive power.St. Mt. 25 v 2 And five of them were wise,and five were foolish.3 They that were foolish took their lamps,and took no oil with them;4 But the wise took oil in their vessels with their lamps.5 While the bridegroom tarried, they all slumbered and slept.Five foolish virgins and five wise. This illustration is talking about a church with the lamp to light the way,but no oil in it to keep it burning.The lamp being the word of God and the oil being the anointing or the presence of God.There are a lot of churches with the word, or the letter of the word, but no spirit or anointing to keep the word activated. When I talk of a wick it is the wick of the flesh being cut or trimmed away.The five wise virgins represent a five fold church with the wisdom to stay in the presence of an all knowing and wise God, by seeking him and resting in his presence. The five foolish represent a church that depends solely on the word of God without keeping the freshness of the anointing or the oil. Without the hand of God rubbing the oil of his presence in our ministries we rely on the letter of the word which is meant to kill the flesh and don't depend the anointing to give to us, the life of God.2nd Co. 3 v. 6 Who also hath made us able ministers of the new testament;not of the letter, but of the spirit;for the letter killeth,but the spirit giveth life.

One in the Spirit

The birthing pains of ministry

I know you are saying what does all of this have do with a female pastor.It is harder,twice as hard, for women to drive these points home in the local church. Although it is bible a lot of things that the holyghost is saying is not taken seriously amongst the local church.Women in high positions in the church have to break through a lot of barriers when there is no backing.And even when there is backing of good leadership,those following the vision and enforcing it;there is often that voice that questions, "does she know the moving of the spirit"? Even as the two wizards, Jan'nes and Jambres withstood Moses as the bible says;so shall these withstand you;2nd Ti. 3 v. 8. We who say we are spiritual are our own greatest critics and henderers.There are those who still think that the church would be better off run by a man and that the women are in the way.God meant for all of these things to come together so the church would be that glorious church spoken of in the book of revelations.The women that God is calling upon in this our have to step up to the plate and do what they do in the spirit and stop making excuses as to why they can't.I n the end when it is all over we too,will have to answer to God.Many are called and yes, few are chosen.And when you are chosen,that means you don't have a say in the matter. It is better to obey.St. John 15 v 16 Ye have not chosen me, but I have chosen you,and ordained you,that ye should go and bring forth fruit,and that your fruit should remain;that whatsoever ye shall ask of the Father in my name,he may give it you.God does the choosing,not us.This is why it is of such a vital degree that we hear from God and do his will. The pioneers we talked about earlier, from Mary,the mother of Jesus,to Debra, the warrior and prophetess.Anna the first preacher to the Jews, to prophetess Bynum. These are our examples of the handy work of God and results of his promise never to forsake us.They paid and some are still paying, a price for women in ministry,but are and were not afraid to break the box.

One in the Spirit

The birthing pains of ministry

Let us look back at Ga. 3 v 22 But the scripture hath concluded all under sin,that the promise by faith of Jesus Christ might be given to them that believe.We examined this passage of scripture earlier as our focus scripture to illuminate our understanding of women and ministry.This scripture reads on to talk about the law,faith and the putting on of Christ or the anointing.It also goes to the closing verse of scripture that opened the revelation of this book up to me.Ga. 3 v 28 There is neither Jew nor Greek,there is neither bond nor free,there is neither male nor female;for ye are all one in Christ Jesus.One in the Spirit.Operating, functioning,growing into the measure of the stature of the perfect man that the bible speaks of. Why would the bible talk about a church being a bride and contradict itself by talking about a church measuring up to the stature of the fullness of Christ.The church has to be equally yoked with the bridegroom in power and perfection.The bride has to be worthy for the groom.It is going to take a people of one mind and one spirit in order to bring her in that place.And a significant role or part of this work, God has ordained for the sisters in the body.It takes a male and a female to create life in the natural and it is going to take male and female,equally in the spirit to bring forth a harvest of souls in this end time hour. Through the eye of God we will see how to teach and mature them and in this process be delivered ourselves.And with the mind of Christ, we will become one ;One in the Spirit.

About the author

At the age of nineteen,Pastor Dixon was called to be a part of the end time church by our Lord Jesus Christ and flowes in the gifts of the spirit.Since aknowledging her call into the realm of prophetic and revelation knowledge.She has a powerful insight to this generation and the timing of the spirit of this age.She has been called to reach the church in this our with a message of unity that she believes will strengthen the growth and development of the end time church.